AF815544

Instability: The Unwitting Effect of Overregulation, The Genius Act, and MiCA (And the Rise of ABTs)

By

Dr. Christopher W. Smithmyer

Elite exclusivity

Dysart Detroit Dallas

© Elite Exclusivity LP and Dr. Christopher Smithmyer 2025
Published by Elite Exclusivity LP
Send all Inquiries to: EliteExclusivityPR@gmail.com and Info@EliteExclusivity.com

ISBN Paperback:
ISBN Hardback:
ISBN Digital:

All Rights Reserved. Except for the Right to Party, which we must fight for. No part of this publication may be reproduced, stored in a retrieval system, or transmitted in any form, electronic, mechanical, photocopying, recording, or otherwise, without the prior written consent of the copyright owners.

Dedication

"When government fears the people, there is liberty. When the people fear the government, there is tyranny."

Attributed to Thomas Jefferson

When we forget this,

Democracy dies.

Use your vote,

Expect Government to Work for You

Replace anyone who has been there more than 10 years.

Table of Contents

Contents

Table of Contents

Table of Contents

Table of Contents

Foreward

When it was announced that the United States was going to pass cryptocurrency legislation in 2024, a sigh of relief went up through the industry. The United States was taking the first step in ensuring that the fastest growing industry worldwide (Web3) would have a set of rules in which to work. The dreamers assumed that the government would bring in the top experts from around the world, or at least around the country, to formulate a law which would be compliant with global movements for greater KYC, AML, and ensure transferability of wealth.

What we got looks like it was ordered off *Wish*. The Genius Act, which was a clever name for a system dumbing down our legislation, should appear in quotes any time that it is used. The Washington elite picked favorites with 10 year out of date technology. Much like the national crypt reserve choosing underperforming assets like XRP, the Genius Act only served to create a OROR oligarchy within the system. Payment Stablecoin technology took a side seat to names politicians new and a complete disregard for *ex post facto* prohibitions in the constitution.

The Genius Act will cripple the United States ability to function in the modern world. The simple process of a bunch of people in a room in Washington challenging already established definitions, even if they use first year law school tools to mask the process seem legitimate, all while they are patting their cronies on the back- read the companies that sponsored the bill, is an affront to the form of government our republic has.

This bill placed stablecoins in the hands of the banks, who during COVID crippled the economy with quantitative easing. Further, they linked a requirement for backing to the US dollar or US dollar related assets. Keep in mind that the United States dollar has lost nearly 30% of its value in the last 5 years.[1] If you look at the last 100 years, the dollar has lost 96% of its purchasing power. AI lists the four major causes of value loss as:

1. The Creation of the Federal Reserve
2. The Great Depression
3. Abolition of Physically Backed Currency
4. Recurring Cycles of Quantitative Easing

Now to put this in perspective, the Genius Act places 90% of stablecoin activity in the hands of Financial Institutions chartered by the Federal Reserve. Expands government overreach, which is one of the key causes of the Great Depression, bans stablecoins based on real world assets and algorithmic stablecoins, and makes “stable” coins dependent on the cycles of quantitative easing promoted by the government!

---

[1] Staff (2025). “United States Inflation Rate.” Trading Economics at https://tradingeconomics.com/united-states/inflation-cpi.

Foreward

I wrote this book to bring the problems to life of the Genius Act, hoping in the next election we can cut off some of the bleeding before it is too late. The "Sunset" clause of the bill allows it to create the real problems about 4 months after the sitting president leaves office- meaning that it is the next guys problem. Hopefully, we can get legislators into place who can protect the American people by eliminating the four problems, mentioned above, from the bill and giving real clarity which promotes innovation.

This book was written quickly, I used the benefit of AI editing to ensure that everything was correct and that a lot of the commentary was removed. Because some of the readers felt that it was a major part of my writing style, I put some of the commentary back in the discussion in sidebars, just to keep things real.

I hope that you enjoy reading this, but even more I hope that you do your own research and help to build a better future.

Preface

If we look at most philosophy, from ancient Hindu text to Christian works, even to Muslim or Animist works we find that there is almost a universal understanding that fear is deadly to the soul. Nearly every major religion in the world presupposes that love and respect for other people is a necessity, even if only at some basic level. We understand that love is a basic opposite of fear; however, in the world in which we live- we allow fear to drive our most basic liberties.

It was once said that a man who would trade liberty for security deserves neither, yet we have entered a political cycle where fear, rather than progress is the terminology of the day. This system allows for abominations, such as the genius act to come into being- not because we “need” the act, but because those in Washington have been taught to fear what would happen if we did not have it.

The Stablecoin methodologies which were put into use 10 years ago, the basis of for the Genius Act of 2025, were great for their time. They were on-ramp/off-ramp tokens for the digital economy (OROR tokens). However, in the last 10 years we have seen more movement in this latest industrial revolution than we have seen in the last 100 years in other sectors. The internet is different. The world is different. But most importantly for this book, Stablecoins are different.

Foreward

This book is a door, it allows you to open your mind to the failings of not just the Genius Act- which is simply a product of cancerous times in world politics- but to the cancer which has been causing decay to society for the last 112 years. Debt based finance has killed the world economy, and we have seen monumental inflation to provide for a "standard of living" which would have made Jules Verne cry and Asimov roll over in his grave. We have the technology to build a better world, but fear has been used to keep us from moving forward.

Case in point, Mr. Elon Musk. First, conservatives hated him. Then Liberals hated him. Then conservatives hated him again. Would it surprise you to know that throughout history, most of the best people were detested by both sides during their lifetime. Christ, Buddha, even Washington lived long enough to be attacked by both political parties. However, some of the worst people stayed loved until their death- mainly because to go against them was suicide. Right now, if you hate Trump or Pelosi you are a "snowflake" or a "MAGA cultist" because we have found it is easier to live in echo chambers than to have real discourse. It is this dynamic within society which has led to the political situation we are in- the situation which produced the Genius Act.

The passage of the act was a failure of our political process. When a sitting president tells members of Congress that they will be primaried if they do not vote for the bill, we have a failure of the republic.

Foreward

When we allow laws that promote ex post facto action, we have a failure of democracy. When we have something so long that few people read it, we have a failure of the education system (a problem for another time). However, the greatest sin of all is when we allow fear of something we do not understand to stifle innovation and progress in the world. Because this can damn us all to a continued hell of debt based finance and withhold a future for which we can all be proud.

Introduction: The laws we neither need or want

“When a management with a reputation for brilliance tackles a business with a reputation for bad economics, it is the reputation of the business that remains intact.”

Warren Buffet[2]

The global financial landscape is in the midst of a profound transformation. For centuries, our economic systems have been built upon a foundation of centralized institutions, sovereign currencies, and physical assets. But with the advent of digital assets and blockchain technology, the very architecture of money and value is undergoing a seismic shift. This digital revolution promises unprecedented efficiency, transparency, and inclusion. Yet, with this promise comes a fundamental challenge: how do we, as regulators and policymakers, navigate this new frontier without stifling the very innovation that drives it? This book is a deep dive into that critical question, exploring two starkly different answers and arguing for a new path forward.

The central conflict is a clash of philosophies. On one side, there is a mindset of preservation—a deep-seated impulse to protect the existing financial order

[2] Staff (2025). “Economics Quotes.” Brainy Quote at https://www.brainyquote.com/topics/economics-quotes.

from the perceived threats of a new and unpredictable technology. This approach views digital assets as a foreign entity to be contained, and its regulatory proposals are designed to fit the digital world into the rigid, outdated molds of the past. It is a philosophy that sees the future not as an opportunity to build something new, but as a problem to be managed.

We have termed this philosophy the “forced conservation of dinosaurs”. The "dinosaurs" are the traditional financial systems—the fiat currencies, the centralized banks, and the incumbent players—that, while once dominant, are now showing their age. "Forced conservation" is the regulatory act of attempting to preserve these systems by preventing the natural evolution of digital money. It is a regulatory posture that, in its bid for familiar safety, inadvertently halts progress and entrenches the very vulnerabilities it claims to protect.

The primary embodiment of this backward-looking philosophy is the GENIUS Act. While its name suggests a forward-thinking approach, the legislation is fundamentally a top-down, prescriptive, and deeply conservative document. It is not an act born of curiosity about the potential of digital assets, but rather one born of a desire to make them behave exactly like their traditional counterparts. It is a classic case of using a new tool to reinforce the old way of doing things.

The most glaring manifestation of this failure is the GENIUS Act’s “fiat-only straitjacket”. By mandating that all regulated stablecoins be 1:1 backed by U.S. dollar-denominated assets, the Act ensures that they are little more than a "blockchain version of a debit card." This approach makes these digital assets inextricably tied to the fate of the U.S. dollar, inheriting all of its vulnerabilities, including its susceptibility to inflation. It is a regulation that, in its pursuit of nominal stability, completely ignores the real-world erosion of purchasing power that every saver experiences.

Furthermore, the GENIUS Act's framework actively discourages the kind of innovation that could lead to a more resilient financial future. Its prohibition on paying interest or yield to stablecoin holders and its high barriers to entry for new issuers are not accidental. They are deliberate mechanisms that protect incumbent institutions from competition and stifle the emergence of what we call "Stablecoin 2.0"—digital assets designed with sophisticated mechanisms to hedge against inflation and offer genuine financial utility. The law, in essence, protects the “dinosaur's moat.”

This book will argue that there is a better path—one that is both more innovative and more secure. This alternative philosophy recognizes that the future of finance lies not in forced conservation, but in digital cooperation. This is a conceptual framework that views digital assets as a powerful tool to be integrated into, and indeed, to improve, our financial systems. It is an approach that builds resilience into the system itself, rather than simply protecting an old system from the new.

This conceptual framework is built on three core pillars that we will explore in detail. The first is a categorized approach to stablecoin regulation, which moves beyond the simple fiat peg to provide a regulated home for a diversity of stability models, including asset-backed and algorithmic systems. This tiered system, inspired by the spirit of the Model Law for Digital Assets (MLDA), is designed to foster innovation while calibrating regulatory oversight to the specific risks of each model.

The second pillar is the critical need to safeguard federal monetary authority. In an era where states might seek to issue their own digital currencies, it is paramount that we prevent a fragmentation of the national monetary system. This framework clarifies the constitutional power of the federal government to coin money, ensuring a unified national currency while still allowing for robust private sector innovation.

The third and final pillar is a proactive and comprehensive approach to financial integrity. This involves a fundamental shift in regulatory focus, mandating universal Know Your Customer (KYC) procedures for all wallet providers and instituting a clear ban on privacy coins. This bold step addresses the long-standing criticisms of illicit finance in the digital asset space, replacing anonymity with accountability and building a more transparent and trustworthy ecosystem for all participants.

Ultimately, this book is a call to action. It is a plea to move beyond the fear of the unknown and to embrace a regulatory philosophy that is as dynamic and innovative as the technology it seeks to govern. The choice before us is a profound one: we can continue down the path of the GENIUS Act, which guarantees a future of financial stagnation and missed opportunity, or we can embrace a framework of digital cooperation, which promises a path toward a more resilient, inclusive, and prosperous digital economy for generations to come. The time for "forced conservation" is over. It is time to give ourselves the permission to move on, to build a future that is not defined by the limitations of the past, but by the boundless potential of the digital age.

Part I: The GENIUS Act

Chapter 1: Permitted Payment Stablecoin Issuers (PPSIs)

"Any competent programmer has an API to cash, payments, escrow, wills, notaries, lotteries, dividends, micropayments, subscriptions, crowdfunding and more."

Naval Ravikant[3]

The passage of the Genius Act was heralded as a triumph of proactive regulation, a framework designed to bring order and safety to the nascent digital assets market.[4] Its centerpiece, the creation of the Permitted Payment Stablecoin Issuer (PPSI), was intended to shield consumers from the systemic risks posed by unbacked stablecoins and to prevent illicit finance from permeating the U.S. financial system. Yet, as we now observe with the benefit of hindsight, the Act's architects were not just reactive but myopic. Their solution, built around a rigid, bank-centric model, was predicated on an outdated understanding of

---

[3] Staff (2025). "Payment Quotes." Brainy Quote at https://www.brainyquote.com/topics/payments-quotes?gad_source=1&gad_campaignid=20728013932&gclid=Cj0KCQjwhafEBhCcARIsAEGZEKIaNQRieKQafyM9l9T2uI0HbjrJjlNYEf-DZPOC17KSHByQVc8MxFEaApBmEALw_wcB

[4] For those of you who read a lot of my work, there are not as many citations in this book. Because the act was written just days before I wrote this, this only citations, other than the government shills promoting the Genius Act, would be from the U.S. Constitution and the Act itself. Rather than bog the book down with thousands of the same citation, I am just putting this note here.

blockchain technology, digital assets, and the very nature of decentralized finance. This chapter will define the PPSI framework, not merely as it was envisioned, but as a monument to regulatory overreach that, in its pursuit of stability, unwittingly fostered a new and far more profound form of instability.

The purported "why" behind the PPSI was compelling on its face: to ensure that any digital asset claiming a one-to-one peg to the U.S. dollar was, in fact, fully backed by high-quality reserves. This addressed the very real concerns of the time, where speculative and algorithmically-backed tokens threatened to cascade into a financial crisis. By requiring full reserve backing and imposing strict prudential standards, the Genius Act sought to guarantee predictable value for users and to mitigate the market manipulation that had plagued the ecosystem. This narrative of consumer protection and systemic risk mitigation provided the political and public justification for a framework that, beneath its veneer of prudence, was designed less for innovation and more for control.

The Genius Act established a bifurcated system for PPSI qualification, allowing both existing Insured Depository Institutions (IDIs) and new, Federal-Qualified Nonbank Issuers to participate. This was a superficial nod to competition. In practice, the rigorous application process and stringent capital requirements created an insurmountable barrier to entry for all but the largest and most established financial entities.

Furthermore, the exclusive right granted to PPSIs to issue stablecoins within the U.S. market, coupled with a "secondary market sunset" for non-compliant tokens, effectively shut out the very innovators who had created the technology. This created an unlevel playing field, cementing the dominance of traditional finance and stifling the organic growth of crypto-native firms.

The rigorous requirements for PPSI qualification, while framed as a necessary measure for financial soundness, were a testament to the legislation's fundamental misunderstanding of the technology it sought to regulate. The mandatory 1:1 reserve mandate and prohibition on rehypothecation were certainly defensible. However, the legislation’s insistence on the PPSI's technical capacity to "seize, freeze, or burn" stablecoins on command revealed a profound disconnect with the ethos of decentralized and censorship-resistant protocols. This centralized kill-switch mechanism, a feature antithetical to the principles of DLT, was a glaring flaw that demonstrated the regulators' desire to exert control over the technology rather than to understand and integrate with it.

Beyond the initial qualification, the ongoing compliance and operational obligations were equally burdensome. PPSIs were designated as financial institutions under the Bank Secrecy Act (BSA), mandating comprehensive AML/KYC programs, transaction monitoring, and SAR reporting. While these measures were necessary, their implementation created a bureaucratic leviathan that favored entities with existing compliance departments and deep pockets. The most damaging constraint, however, was the outright ban on PPSIs paying interest or yield to stablecoin holders. This single provision, intended to prevent risky banking activities, acted as a direct prohibition on the core functionality of decentralized finance (DeFi), severing the link between stablecoins and the most innovative use cases of the era.

The long-term impact of the PPSI framework was predictable and profound. By erecting such high barriers to entry, the Genius Act consolidated the stablecoin market around a handful of traditional financial institutions. The promise of a dynamic and competitive ecosystem was replaced by a rigid oligopoly. This regulatory-induced ossification did more than just stifle domestic innovation; it actively drove it offshore. The most creative and resourceful developers, facing a choice between a sterile, heavily regulated market and a dynamic, permissive global landscape, took their talent and capital elsewhere. The U.S., which had the opportunity to lead in the development of open, permissionless financial infrastructure, instead became a bystander to its own self-inflicted decline.

This chapter, therefore, will not simply define the PPSI. It will serve as a detailed and critical autopsy of the framework, meticulously examining how its design, requirements, and prohibitions, far from securing the digital asset market, laid the groundwork for its most significant instability. By creating a system that prioritized centralized control over technological integrity and innovation, the Genius Act ironically accelerated the flight from regulated fiat-backed stablecoins toward more resilient, truly decentralized alternatives—a phenomenon that ultimately culminated in the rise of Asset-Backed Tokens (ABTs), the very technology the Act's authors had failed to foresee.

Defining the Permitted Payment Stablecoin Issuer (PPSI)

The regulatory rationale for the PPSI framework, as codified in the Genius Act, was rooted in a tri-pronged approach to financial stability and consumer protection. First and foremost, it sought to address the systemic risks posed by a rapidly expanding ecosystem of largely unbacked or undercollateralized stablecoins. The fear was a domino effect where a "bank run" on a large, under-reserved token could destabilize other digital asset markets, potentially spilling over into traditional finance. Secondly, the Act aimed to ensure predictable value for users by mandating a strict 1:1 reserve requirement, a seemingly unassailable principle given the failures of a few prominent algorithmic stablecoins. Lastly, the framework was positioned as a bulwark against illicit finance and market manipulation, leveraging the regulatory infrastructure of traditional banking to enforce robust anti-money laundering (AML) and sanctions compliance. While these objectives were certainly laudable, the Act's approach to achieving them was fundamentally flawed, a classic example of "fighting the last war" by attempting to retroactively apply legacy regulatory models to a decentralized, forward-looking technology.

The Genius Act, in its effort to foster a competitive yet controlled environment, created three distinct categories for PPSI qualification: subsidiaries of Insured Depository Institutions (IDIs), Federal-Qualified Nonbank Issuers, and State-Qualified Nonbank Issuers. This tiered structure was presented as an inclusive pathway for both established financial players and emerging fintech firms. IDI subsidiaries were positioned to leverage existing banking infrastructure, capital, and regulatory oversight, giving them a significant head start. Federal-qualified nonbanks, meanwhile, were ostensibly the new frontier for crypto-native firms, offering a path to operate on a national scale. Lastly, state-qualified nonbanks were intended to provide a more localized, state-level regulatory option. However, this seemingly open-door policy was a red herring. In practice, the application process, capital burdens, and ongoing compliance costs were so prohibitive that they effectively created a high-walled fortress, accessible only to the most well-capitalized institutions, thereby stifling genuine competition and market dynamism.

The most controversial and consequential element of the Genius Act was the explicit grant of an exclusive right to PPSIs for stablecoin issuance within the United States. This provision, coupled with a "secondary market sunset" that prohibited the trading of non-compliant tokens after a specified period, was the regulatory equivalent of a surgical strike on the entire stablecoin ecosystem that existed prior to the Act. This move effectively banned a wide range of popular, established, and foreign-issued stablecoins from the U.S. market, forcing a massive, government-mandated consolidation. The implications were immediate and severe, forcing many existing stablecoin projects to either cease U.S. operations or pursue the onerous and likely futile path of PPSI qualification. It was this singular provision that demonstrated the legislation's true intent: not to integrate digital assets into the financial system, but to subsume and control them under a traditional, centralized model, a decision that would have far-reaching and unintended consequences for the future of digital finance.

The Rigorous Requirements for PPSI Qualification

The Genius Act's PPSI framework was not merely a new set of rules but a fortress built with deliberately high walls. The requirements for qualification were so stringent that they effectively served as a de facto entry barrier, ensuring that only the largest and most well-capitalized institutions could even contemplate becoming a PPSI. This section will dissect these requirements, revealing how each provision, while presented as a safeguard, was a deliberate constraint on innovation and a subtle mechanism for market consolidation.

The application and approval process was a bureaucratic gauntlet designed to favor incumbents. Prospective issuers were required to submit extensive, often proprietary, documentation to a federal or state regulator, a process demanding significant legal and compliance resources. The evaluation criteria—centered on financial soundness, operational integrity, and management competence—were direct imports from traditional banking supervision, which, by their very nature, penalized the lean, agile structures of fintech startups. In the state regime, the Stablecoin Certification Review Committee (SCRC) added an additional layer of complexity, introducing a multi-jurisdictional approval process that was as opaque as it was time-consuming. This convoluted pathway ensured that by the time an application was considered, the applicant had already spent millions and likely months, if not years, in a regulatory holding pattern, an investment few crypto-native firms could afford.

At the core of the PPSI framework were the capital, liquidity, and risk management standards, which represented a full-scale transposition of prudential oversight from traditional finance to the digital asset space. This included mandatory capital requirements that were sized to the volume and risk profile of the stablecoin being issued, a framework that, while superficially logical, was a disproportionate burden for any entity not already operating with a multi-billion dollar balance sheet. Additionally, PPSIs were mandated to implement comprehensive risk management frameworks covering operational, cybersecurity, and even interest rate risks. While cybersecurity concerns were paramount and well-justified, the imposition of traditional interest rate risk models on a non-interest-bearing digital asset demonstrated a clear lack of understanding of the underlying technology's mechanics and a slavish adherence to outdated regulatory playbooks.

The Genius Act’s most widely praised feature was the 1:1 reserve mandate, a direct response to the era of algorithmic stablecoins and under-reserved digital assets. This provision required that every stablecoin in circulation be fully backed by High-Quality Liquid Assets (HQLAs) such as U.S. Treasury bills and cash. To further protect against a crisis, the Act included a strict prohibition on rehypothecation of reserves, ensuring that these backing assets could not be used for any other purpose. This was a sound principle, yet the Act went further, excluding a wide range of assets, from corporate debt and equities to other cryptocurrencies. While this minimized risk in the short term, it also severely limited the PPSI’s ability to use a broader and more diverse set of collateral, a foundational principle of the decentralized lending protocols that were gaining traction at the time.

Perhaps the most revealing aspect of the Genius Act’s flawed design was its requirements for operational readiness and technical capabilities. While maintaining robust systems for issuance and redemption was a basic necessity, the inclusion of a requirement for PPSIs to have the capacity to "seize, freeze, or burn" stablecoins under lawful directives was a stunning admission of the Act's centralizing philosophy. This feature, antithetical to the very idea of a decentralized, permissionless ledger, represented a gross misunderstanding of blockchain’s immutability and resistance to censorship. It was a technical backdoor, designed to give regulators ultimate control and thereby subvert the core promise of DLT. This provision, alongside the mandates for secure private key management and blockchain integration, showcased a desire to put traditional regulatory reins on a technology fundamentally designed to operate without them.

Ongoing Compliance and Operational Obligations of PPSIs

The Genius Act's PPSI framework extended far beyond a one-time qualification, imposing a continuous set of compliance and operational obligations that further entrenched the dominance of traditional financial institutions and acted as a constant drag on innovation. These requirements, while framed as necessary for ongoing stability, created a regulatory treadmill that was simply too fast for most agile, crypto-native firms to keep pace with.

The transparency and disclosure requirements of the Genius Act, while seemingly beneficial for market participants, created a significant and perpetual operational burden. PPSIs were mandated to provide monthly public attestations of reserve composition, a process that necessitated the continuous engagement of third-party auditors and lawyers to ensure accuracy and compliance. These attestations, along with mandatory third-party audits by registered public accounting firms, became a costly ritual, cementing the market advantage of institutions with existing relationships and resources for such work. Furthermore, the requirement for publicly available redemption policies with clear fee structures provided a veneer of consumer protection while simultaneously locking PPSIs into rigid, hard-to-adapt business models, unable to quickly respond to market changes or competitive pressures.

In a move that sealed the fate of the PPSI as a crypto-native non-starter, the Genius Act classified all issuers as "financial institutions" under the Bank Secrecy Act (BSA). This designation triggered a cascade of regulatory obligations, including the implementation of robust Anti-Money Laundering (AML) and Know Your Customer (KYC) programs, comprehensive transaction monitoring, and a rigorous process for Suspicious Activity Report (SAR) reporting. While these measures are a cornerstone of preventing illicit finance, their application to the PPSI framework represented an expensive and complex undertaking that only large, established financial entities could seamlessly integrate. This regulatory hurdle, far from fostering responsible innovation, simply disqualified smaller, more nimble firms from the start.

The section on prohibited activities and business model constraints stands out as the most damaging and shortsighted provision of the Genius Act. The outright ban on paying interest or yield to stablecoin holders solely for holding was a direct assault on the core mechanics of decentralized finance (DeFi). This single rule, intended to prevent the kind of risky, fractional-reserve lending that precipitated past financial crises, effectively made stablecoins a dead-end asset class for any meaningful on-chain composability or yield generation. The prohibition on "tying" arrangements, which prevented the bundling of stablecoins with other products, and the severe limitations on non-financial commercial firms acting as PPSIs further crippled potential business models. These constraints, born from a traditional banking mindset, utterly failed to comprehend that a stablecoin's value in the digital economy was derived not from its static nature, but from its dynamic utility within a broader ecosystem of lending, trading, and decentralized applications.

Finally, the consumer protections and marketing guidelines of the Act, while well-intentioned, added another layer of rigidity. The prohibition on misrepresenting stablecoins as government-backed or federally insured was a crucial and necessary safeguard against fraud. However, the mandate for clear and conspicuous redemption procedures and the requirement for safeguarding customer funds through asset segregation simply codified standard banking practices into the digital asset space. While ensuring the safety of user funds is paramount, the manner in which it was enforced demonstrated a fundamental lack of trust in the technology's ability to create trust through cryptographic guarantees rather than through centralized, bureaucratic oversight. In effect, the Act demanded that digital assets behave exactly like traditional bank deposits, completely ignoring the unique architectural advantages and possibilities of the underlying technology.

The Impact and Future Landscape for PPSIs

The Genius Act, a monumental legislative effort to regulate the stablecoin market, had a profound and immediate impact that reverberated through the financial ecosystem. The framework's design, far from creating a level playing field, had a highly predictable outcome: market consolidation. By creating an environment of exorbitant barriers to entry, from the complex application process to the astronomical capital requirements, the Act gave a decisive advantage to traditional financial institutions and large, well-resourced entities. The very same institutions it was meant to protect against were handed the keys to the kingdom. Conversely, smaller fintechs and crypto-native startups, the very source of innovation, faced insurmountable challenges. This created a landscape where the most dynamic and creative firms were sidelined, and the market was dominated by a handful of established players. The inevitable result was a significant reduction in innovation, as the competitive pressure that fuels technological advancement was replaced by a rigid oligopoly of PPSIs.

The Genius Act did not exist in a vacuum; its framework had a complex and often contradictory interplay with existing regulatory frameworks. The legislation's most significant "carrot" was the explicit exemption from securities and commodities classification for compliant PPSIs, a move intended to provide regulatory clarity and certainty. However, this clarity came at the cost of a new, complex regulatory structure. The Act's provisions had to be carefully navigated alongside existing state money transmitter laws, creating a patchwork of legal obligations for PPSIs operating across different jurisdictions. Furthermore, the Genius Act created a new bureaucratic apparatus in the Stablecoin Certification Review Committee (SCRC), whose role was to coordinate with federal banking agencies and other regulators. This created a new layer of friction and potential for regulatory capture, rather than the streamlined, efficient process that was originally promised.

The Genius Act's approach to foreign issuers and cross-border considerations was a clear reflection of its protectionist and control-oriented philosophy. To operate in the U.S., foreign stablecoin issuers were required to meet the same stringent PPSI standards as domestic firms. This created a massive disincentive for global players to enter the U.S. market. The decision for a foreign issuer to be "comparable" was left to the sole discretion of the Treasury Secretary, a political and subjective determination that introduced an element of unpredictability into a market that craved certainty. While the Genius Act ostensibly created an opportunity for the U.S. to lead in global stablecoin interoperability, its parochial, inward-looking design made such a vision impossible. Instead, it served to isolate the U.S. market, creating a segregated system that was out of step with the global, permissionless nature of DLT.

In its long-term vision, the Genius Act presented a stark choice: was it truly fostering responsible innovation, or was it simply stifling growth? The legislation's champions argued that by balancing financial stability with market dynamism, the Act would create a safe and trusted ecosystem for digital assets. They envisioned the U.S. becoming a leader in regulated stablecoins, a beacon of stability in a volatile global market. Yet, in practice, the Act's heavy-handed approach and its reliance on outdated technological assumptions created significant risks of driving innovation offshore. The most talented developers and the most creative projects, confronted with an inhospitable U.S. regulatory climate, simply took their work elsewhere. Ultimately, the Genius Act, in its obsessive pursuit of control, ironically drove the very instability it sought to prevent, by pushing the most innovative segments of the digital asset market into the unregulated shadows and laying the groundwork for the rise of a new class of decentralized assets it had failed to even comprehend.

Conclusion

In hindsight, the Genius Act stands as a powerful cautionary tale, a testament to the unintended consequences of well-meaning but ill-informed regulation. Its primary ambition—to create a stable and safe digital asset market—was a noble one. Yet, by approaching a revolutionary technology with a legacy regulatory playbook, the Act's architects inadvertently sowed the seeds of a new and more complex form of instability. The Permitted Payment Stablecoin Issuer (PPSI) framework, as we have detailed, was not a bridge to the future of finance but a regulatory wall built to contain a market that was fundamentally decentralized and global. The irony is inescapable: a law designed to prevent a crisis of confidence in stablecoins ultimately created a crisis of confidence in regulated digital assets themselves.

The PPSI framework's design was fundamentally rooted in a pre-blockchain mindset. It attempted to retroactively fit a decentralized, permissionless technology into a centralized, permissioned structure. The tiered system of PPSI qualification, the rigid prudential standards, and the exclusive right to issue were not innovations but rather defensive measures to protect the existing financial order. In doing so, the Genius Act failed to recognize that the most significant value of digital assets lies not in their ability to mimic existing financial instruments, but in their capacity to enable entirely new forms of economic interaction. It was a failure of imagination, a regulatory framework that looked backward instead of forward.

Among the most damaging provisions were the financial and operational requirements, which were designed to mirror those of traditional banks. The exorbitant capital mandates and the ban on paying yield to stablecoin holders acted as a direct, almost surgical, strike against the nascent decentralized finance (DeFi) ecosystem. DeFi's promise was to use digital assets to build transparent, programmatic financial services without the need for costly intermediaries. The Genius Act, by prohibiting yield and mandating expensive, centralized compliance, effectively criminalized the very business models that were driving innovation, ensuring that a compliant PPSI would be a static, uncompetitive, and ultimately irrelevant asset within the broader digital economy.

The Genius Act's most profound philosophical error was codified in the technical requirement that PPSIs must have the capacity to "seize, freeze, or burn" stablecoins. This provision, a clear attempt to impose state-level control on a decentralized technology, was a direct contradiction of blockchain's foundational principles of immutability and censorship resistance. It demonstrated a profound misunderstanding of the technology's ethos and a prioritization of centralized authority over cryptographic integrity. This single mandate, more than any other, signaled to the global digital asset community that the U.S. was more interested in controlling the technology than in embracing its potential for creating a more resilient and transparent financial system.

The inevitable consequence was a complete restructuring of the digital asset market, but not in the way the regulators had intended. The high barriers to entry and the hostile regulatory environment for native crypto firms drove the most innovative projects and talented developers offshore. The U.S. stablecoin market became a static, centralized oligopoly, dominated by a handful of large financial institutions whose products were functionally indistinguishable from one another. Meanwhile, outside of the U.S. jurisdiction, the experimentation and innovation continued unabated, leading to the development of new, more resilient protocols and assets that were beyond the reach of the Genius Act's regulatory grasp.

This exodus of talent and capital created the very vacuum the book's title alludes to. By stifling the growth of regulated, fiat-backed stablecoins and alienating the DeFi community, the Genius Act unintentionally accelerated the search for a new, truly decentralized alternative. As we will explore in the subsequent chapters, this search culminated in the rise of Asset-Backed Tokens (ABTs)—digital assets whose value is derived not from a centralized issuer's promise, but from the immutable, on-chain fractional ownership of real-world, productive assets. The Genius Act did not kill the stablecoin; it simply forced it to evolve into a form that was more resilient, more decentralized, and entirely beyond its control.

Chapter 2: Mandatory 1:1 Reserve Backing with "High Quality" Liquid Assets (HQLAs) and Prohibition of Yield

"One way to ease liquidity for banks is that the government can buy all highly rated securities held by the banks. Every single bank in the UAE has some sovereign debts held in their portfolios. I am not asking them to buy any junk bonds, rather the high quality UAE government debt."

Abdul Aziz Al Ghurair[5]

The Genius Act, in its effort to impose order on the nascent digital asset market, was defined by two central pillars: the mandatory **1:1 reserve backing** for all Permitted Payment Stablecoins (PPSIs) and the explicit **prohibition of interest or yield** on those tokens. These provisions were not merely technical requirements but were the ideological and operational core of the entire framework. They represented a direct application of traditional banking and monetary principles to a fundamentally new technology, a decision made with the best of intentions but with a profound misunderstanding of the innovation it sought to regulate. This chapter will meticulously dissect these two mandates, arguing that while they were designed to forge a foundation of trust, they instead created an environment of regulatory-induced

[5] Staff (2025). "Liquidity Quotes." Brainy Quote at https://www.brainyquote.com/topics/liquidity-quotes.

stagnation that ultimately pushed the market toward more dynamic and less-regulated alternatives.

The rationale behind the strict reserve requirements was, on its face, entirely defensible. The collapses of unbacked, algorithmic stablecoins had created genuine fear of "digital bank runs" and a potential spillover of systemic risk. The Genius Act's mandate for every stablecoin to be redeemable at par for fiat currency and backed by a 1:1 reserve of high-quality liquid assets (HQLAs) was presented as the ultimate safeguard against such failures. It was a direct response to past market chaos, but it was a response that treated the symptom, not the underlying condition. By focusing exclusively on the reserve mechanism, the Act’s framers ignored the other, more powerful use cases for these assets, effectively constraining their utility to that of a simple digital dollar.

The definition of a Permitted Reserve Universe was deliberately and unapologetically narrow. The Act's framers designated only U.S. currency, short-term Treasury securities, and demand deposits at insured banks as HQLAs. This conservative approach, while admirable from a pure risk-mitigation standpoint, was a significant miscalculation from a market-dynamics perspective. It explicitly **prohibited a vast array of assets**—from commercial paper to equities and, most importantly, other cryptocurrencies—from being used as backing collateral. This choice, born out of a desire for extreme stability, not only removed potential for diversification but also completely severed the PPSI from the very on-chain financial ecosystem it was meant to service.

Perhaps the most controversial and consequential decision of the Genius Act was the explicit prohibition of interest or yield. This rule was a direct response to the perceived threat of stablecoins becoming a form of "shadow banking," a worry that PPSIs might become a source of unbacked lending and competition with traditional bank deposits. While the intention was to prevent risk, the impact was to render the PPSI framework functionally useless for the most innovative and rapidly growing sectors of digital finance. By making it illegal to pay a yield, the Act eliminated the primary incentive for holding stablecoins within a decentralized context, where every asset is expected to be a productive one.

This dual-pronged regulatory approach—strict, conservative reserves combined with a prohibition on yield—created a paradox. The Genius Act promised to build public trust in stablecoins by making them as safe as traditional banking products, yet in doing so, it rendered them economically unattractive and technically sterile within the digital ecosystem. The high cost of maintaining a non-yielding, regulated asset, coupled with the opportunity cost for holders, made PPSIs a non-starter for the very institutional investors and applications that were driving the market forward.

This chapter examines the precise legal and operational implications of these rules. We will explore how the rigid HQLA requirement and the anti-yield provision not only shaped the compliant stablecoin market but also created a powerful incentive for market participants to seek alternative, unregulated solutions. It is in this regulatory void, created by the Genius Act's conservative oversight, that we will see the true and unwitting genius of the market: the development of new, productive digital assets that exist entirely outside the PPSI framework.

Strict Reserves

The Genius Act's most touted provision was the mandate for a 1:1 reserve backing, a direct and visceral response to the era of algorithmic stablecoin collapses that had shaken the market. The rationale, as articulated by the Act's proponents, was to prevent a repeat of these failures by ensuring that every digital dollar token was, in fact, fully backed by real-world assets. This was framed as a necessary measure to mitigate systemic risk, to prevent "digital bank runs," and to build a bedrock of public trust that had been eroded by speculative failures. However, this approach, while seemingly prudent, was also profoundly reactive. It focused on solving a problem of the past while entirely missing the opportunity to design a forward-looking system. In its zealous pursuit of a perfect, static balance sheet, the Act's framers failed to recognize that a stablecoin's true utility was not in its passive reserve but in its dynamic application within the broader digital economy.

Integral to the strict reserve framework was the definition of a 1:1 redemption obligation. Under the Genius Act, every stablecoin issued by a Permitted Payment Stablecoin Issuer (PPSI) was required to be redeemable "at par" for fiat currency on a moment's notice. This legal commitment to immediate convertibility was intended to ensure a predictable value for users under all market conditions, thereby making the PPSI a credible and trustworthy medium of exchange. It was a seemingly unassailable principle, mirroring the promise of a traditional money market fund. Yet, in practice, this requirement, combined with the Act’s other provisions, created a fragile and rigid system. By enshrining immediate, fiat-based redemption as the sole metric of a stablecoin’s success, the Act effectively discouraged the development of new, more sophisticated redemption and collateral models that were already being explored by innovators in the decentralized finance (DeFi) space.

Perhaps the most economically consequential of the Genius Act's provisions was the explicit prohibition of interest or yield on PPSI stablecoins. This rule was intended to draw a clear line of demarcation, distinguishing stablecoins from interest-bearing deposits or securities and, most importantly, addressing concerns about "shadow banking." The framers feared that if stablecoins were to pay a yield, they would become a source of unbacked lending, creating a new, unregulated credit market that could destabilize the financial system. However, this absolute ban proved to be a fatal flaw. It made PPSIs a non-starter for the very users and applications that were driving the growth of the digital asset economy. By rendering the PPSI a sterile, non-productive asset, the Act guaranteed its marginalization and rendered it uncompetitive with a burgeoning international market of yield-bearing tokenized instruments.

High-Quality Liquid Assets (HQLAs): The Permitted Reserve Universe

The Genius Act's strict reserve mandate was given its substance by a very specific and narrow definition of High-Quality Liquid Assets (HQLAs). The Act's framers, drawing heavily from traditional banking frameworks like Basel III, defined these assets by three core characteristics: they must have low credit risk, high liquidity, and stable valuation. This meant that the assets had to be government-backed or highly-rated, easily convertible to cash with minimal loss, and possess low price volatility even under periods of market stress. The intent was clear: to create a pool of assets so safe and so liquid that a PPSI could, in theory, withstand a full-scale digital bank run without a single blip. Yet, this conservative approach, while admirable from a pure risk-mitigation standpoint, was a masterclass in regulatory minimalism, intentionally ignoring the more dynamic and innovative forms of collateral that were already emerging in the digital asset space.

The Permitted Reserve Asset Classes under the Genius Act were therefore a predictable and uninspired list. They included U.S. currency, demand deposits at insured depository institutions, short-term U.S. Treasury securities (with maturities of 93 days or less), and overnight repurchase agreements (repos) collateralized by these same HQLAs. This narrow universe of acceptable assets created a regulatory safe zone that was effectively an extension of the traditional financial system. By confining PPSIs to these specific instruments, the Act's framers ensured that stablecoin reserves would remain fully within the purview and control of traditional central banking and governmental debt markets. It was a framework designed to make stablecoins behave exactly like money market funds, a static and unyielding paradigm that was ill-suited for the innovative, on-chain financial applications that were gaining traction at the time.

The Act's philosophy was even more explicitly revealed in its list of prohibited reserve assets. The Genius Act explicitly excluded commercial paper, corporate bonds, and equities, deeming them too risky for stablecoin reserves. This was a direct rebuke of the private credit markets and the broader equity landscape. Most tellingly, however, was the outright ban on other cryptocurrencies or commodity-backed assets. This particular restriction demonstrated a profound lack of trust in the digital asset ecosystem itself, preventing PPSIs from diversifying their reserves with other digital assets or from creating more sophisticated collateral models. This regulatory exclusion not only stifled innovation but also created an artificial and fragile boundary between the compliant PPSI market and the burgeoning, more dynamic universe of decentralized, cryptographically-backed assets.

Safeguarding Reserves: Custody, Segregation, and Verification

The Genius Act's approach to safeguarding reserves, while superficially sound, was predicated on an economic model that utterly failed to leverage the advantages of distributed ledger technology (DLT). By mandating traditional, off-chain methods of custody and verification, the system undermined the very principles of transparency and capital efficiency that good economics demands. This section will dissect how each of these provisions, in a misguided attempt to mirror legacy finance, became a mechanism for economic inefficiency and a powerful incentive to seek alternatives.

The requirement for segregation of customer assets was a prime example of this flawed logic. While a cornerstone of investor protection in traditional finance—where co-mingling of funds is a major risk—its application to a DLT-based system was economically counterproductive. In the world of centralized banking, segregation prevents fraud and protects consumers in the event of insolvency.

However, on a distributed ledger, cryptographic proof of asset ownership and reserve status can be provided in real-time, programmatically, and immutably. The Genius Act's insistence on off-chain segregation not only created a regulatory burden but also ignored the potential for a more robust, transparent, and provable on-chain solution. It created a system where assets were treated as static, isolated entities, instead of dynamic components of a global, verifiable ledger.

Similarly, the imposition of qualified custody requirements created an economic bottleneck that stifled innovation. By mandating the use of regulated and supervised custodians, the Genius Act effectively created a new, centralized choke point in a market that was supposed to be decentralized. This provision handed a monopoly on custody to a handful of large, established players, while simultaneously disincentivizing the development of new, more secure, and potentially more efficient custody solutions native to the digital asset space, such as multi-signature wallets and decentralized custodianship models. A more effective methodology can be seen in the requirements of third-party custody under the Cerberus © tokenization methodology. The economic cost of this provision was a lack of competition, a perpetuation of high-cost services, and the reintroduction of single points of failure that the blockchain was designed to eliminate.

The regulations surrounding transparency, attestations, and audits were a performative exercise in economic inefficiency. The Genius Act mandated monthly public disclosures of reserve composition, along with independent third-party attestations and CEO/CFO certifications. While these measures were intended to build trust, they did so in a time-delayed, costly, and ultimately limited fashion. The entire system was a bureaucratic ritual that was economically inferior to the real-time, on-chain transparency that a well-designed DLT could provide. Instead of leveraging the cryptographic certainty of a distributed ledger, the Act chose to rely on the costly and human-intensive process of auditing, a system that provided a snapshot of the past rather than a continuous, verifiable truth.

The most egregious economic error of the Genius Act, however, was its prohibition on rehypothecation. This rule, intended to ensure that reserves were truly 1:1 and immediately available, was a fundamental misunderstanding of how capital creates value. In a traditional financial system, rehypothecation, while carrying risks, is a key mechanism for creating liquidity and velocity. The Genius Act, in its obsessive pursuit of a "safe and sound" stablecoin, created an asset that was perfectly safe but also perfectly sterile. By preventing the re-use or lending of reserves, it eliminated any incentive for capital efficiency, turning billions of dollars into a non-productive, dormant pool of assets. This economic flaw was a primary driver for the rise of Asset-Backed Tokens (ABTs), which were designed to solve this very problem by allowing capital to be both verifiably reserved and programmatically productive.

Market Implications and Scalability Challenges

The Genius Act, through its strict reserve and anti-yield provisions, fundamentally altered the economic calculus for market participants. The most immediate and significant consequence was the introduction of a substantial cost to holding non-yielding assets. For large institutional holders and corporates, the opportunity cost of parking capital in a PPSI stablecoin was immense. This created a powerful disincentive for holding stablecoins for extended periods beyond immediate payment needs, as their capital was effectively dormant. The Genius Act's rigid framework inadvertently created a powerful incentive for a shift of capital to yield-bearing tokenized instruments elsewhere, particularly in foreign jurisdictions or within the less-regulated corners of the decentralized finance (DeFi) ecosystem. This was a clear example of regulatory arbitrage, where capital flows to where it is most productively employed, entirely bypassing the sterile environment of the PPSI.

The stringent requirements also had a profound impact on stablecoin business models. With the primary revenue stream of interest on reserves eliminated, issuers were forced to shift their revenue models from interest on reserves to fees for services.

This meant PPSIs had to rely on transaction fees, foreign exchange fees, or other service-based charges to remain profitable. This created significant challenges for issuers to remain profitable and invest in infrastructure, as the scalability of a fee-based model is inherently more complex than one built on passive interest income. While this did encourage efficiency in operations and transaction-based services, it also fundamentally transformed the stablecoin from a passive, stable asset into a service-oriented product, limiting its utility as a foundational building block for other financial applications.

The Genius Act created an interesting and fraught competition with traditional bank deposits. By creating a regulated, non-interest-bearing alternative to traditional deposits, the Act introduced a new variable into the financial system. There were immediate concerns about potential "deposit flight" from traditional banks, as institutional and corporate capital could, in theory, move from FDIC-insured accounts to PPSIs. This concern, while significant, was ultimately mitigated by the fundamental distinction between the two: the role of FDIC insurance for traditional deposits versus stablecoin backing. While a PPSI's 1:1 reserve was intended to guarantee stability, it lacked the full faith and credit of the U.S. government, a psychological and systemic backstop that traditional deposits enjoyed. The PPSI was therefore positioned not as a true competitor to traditional deposits, but as a niche payment vehicle for digital asset markets.

In the long-term, the PPSI framework's most profound effect was on scalability and innovation. The Act's architects chose to foster a more "secure" but potentially less dynamic stablecoin market, a direct result of the trade-off between strict stability and rapid widespread adoption. By prioritizing a conservative, bank-like model, the U.S. framework rendered itself uncompetitive on the global stage. As other jurisdictions, with more permissive regulatory regimes, allowed for yield-bearing stablecoins and more innovative collateral models, the U.S. became a market of one. The Genius Act's rigid framework, with its explicit anti-yield stance, created a powerful disincentive for global adoption and ultimately became an international outlier, proving that a myopic focus on stability can ultimately lead to a loss of relevance and a flight of innovation.

Conclusion

Chapter 2 has examined the foundational pillars of the Genius Act's PPSI framework: the mandatory 1:1 reserve backing and the prohibition of yield. While these regulations were born from a desire for stability and consumer protection, our analysis reveals they were deeply flawed, a case of regulatory overcorrection that mistook the symptom for the disease. By applying an archaic, bank-centric model to a dynamic and global technology, the Genius Act didn't just constrain the stablecoin market; it actively distorted it, setting the stage for the very instability it was created to prevent. The Act's insistence on a sterile, non-productive asset class was its most profound and lasting miscalculation.

The reserve requirements, while sound in principle, were overly rigid and conservative in practice. The Genius Act's narrow definition of High-Quality Liquid Assets (HQLAs) and its absolute prohibition on rehypothecation, while aimed at mitigating risk, failed to appreciate the full potential of distributed ledger technology (DLT). By forbidding PPSIs from using a broader range of assets or from leveraging their reserves in a transparent, programmatic way, the Act forced them into a static and inefficient model. It completely missed the opportunity to create a new form of capital efficiency, where reserves could be cryptographically proven and used in novel ways without compromising the 1:1 redemption promise.

However, it was the prohibition of yield that proved to be the most critical and damaging flaw. This single rule, intended to shield consumers from the risks of "shadow banking," had the unintended effect of making PPSIs an economically unattractive asset within the digital economy. In a world of decentralized finance where capital is expected to be productive, a non-yielding stablecoin is a dead-end. The Act's framers failed to grasp that the utility of a digital asset is not just its function as a medium of exchange, but its ability to be seamlessly integrated into a complex ecosystem of lending, borrowing, and trading. By severing this connection, the Genius Act rendered the

PPSI framework irrelevant to the very market it was meant to serve.

The immediate market implications were predictable and profound. The Genius Act created a two-tiered stablecoin ecosystem: a small, regulated, non-yielding market of PPSIs and a burgeoning, international, and largely unregulated market of yield-bearing stablecoins and other digital assets. Capital, ever in search of the highest risk-adjusted return, flowed out of the sterile PPSI environment and into these more dynamic, globally accessible protocols. This created a dangerous paradox: the regulatory framework that promised to create a safe, domestic stablecoin market instead created a powerful incentive for domestic capital to seek riskier, less-transparent opportunities offshore.

Ultimately, the Genius Act's myopic focus on stability through a rigid, non-yielding framework was a masterclass in unintentional consequences. By creating a stablecoin that was safe but sterile, it directly catalyzed the market's flight towards new, innovative forms of value. It was this regulatory vacuum, this deliberate refusal to integrate with the core mechanics of decentralized finance, that set the stage for the rise of Asset-Backed Tokens (ABTs). As we will explore, these new tokens offered a solution to the very problems the Genius Act created, but did so entirely outside of its regulatory reach, proving that innovation, once unleashed, will always find a way to flourish beyond the confines of outdated regulation.

Chapter 3: Reporting, Disclosure and Audits

"Uncontrolled access to data, with no audit trail of activity and no oversight would be going too far. This applies both to commercial and government use of data about people."

John Poindexter[6]

In the wake of past stablecoin failures and the pervasive narrative of an unregulated "Wild West," the Genius Act's provisions for reporting, disclosure, and audits were presented as a powerful remedy. They were the very mechanisms intended to restore public trust, provide rigorous regulatory oversight, and cement the credibility of U.S.-issued stablecoins on the global stage. This chapter will delve into these provisions, not to praise their intentions, but to dissect their practical and economic consequences. We will argue that while these requirements created a facade of transparency, they were in fact a costly and inefficient system, a clear example of regulators choosing a familiar but flawed off-chain solution over the more robust, real-time, and cryptographic

[6] Staff (2025). "Audit Quotes." Brainy Quote at https://www.brainyquote.com/topics/audit-quotes?gad_source=1&gad_campaignid=20728013932&gclid=Cj0KCQjwhafEBhCcARIsAEGZEKIHNP-ZHAPAqrrSUtL8Wpe4oEz1OUppf8r_kJouI2N70Xa1KIazAo4aAgEPEALw_wcB.

transparency inherent to distributed ledger technology (DLT).

The rationale for this regulatory approach was clear: to address the historical lack of transparency that had plagued the stablecoin market. By mandating monthly public disclosures of reserve composition and subjecting issuers to independent third-party audits, the Act sought to combat misrepresentation and fraud. The goal was to ensure that every PPSI's claim of a 1:1 reserve was not a matter of trust but of verifiable, audited fact. This approach, however, was fundamentally a step backward. Instead of embracing the cryptographic proof that a distributed ledger could provide, the Genius Act chose to rely on the costly and time-delayed processes of legacy auditing, a system that provided a snapshot of the past rather than a continuous, verifiable truth.

These reporting and disclosure requirements were also a central pillar of the Act's strategy for regulatory oversight and risk monitoring. The comprehensive financial statements and operational reports were intended to give regulators a clear, real-time picture of an issuer's solvency and to identify potential systemic risks. Yet, this reliance on periodic, human-intensive reporting created a regulatory blind spot. In a market where digital bank runs can happen in minutes, a monthly or quarterly report is an artifact of history, not a tool for real-time risk management. The Act's framers were so focused on the mechanics of traditional oversight that they entirely missed the opportunity to build a new, more effective regulatory framework based on on-chain data and automated, programmatic monitoring.

The Genius Act's auditing requirements, in particular, represented a significant victory for the traditional financial establishment and a loss for innovation. By mandating monthly third-party attestations by Public Company Accounting Oversight Board (PCAOB) registered firms and annual audits for large issuers, the Act made the legacy auditing industry a mandatory and highly profitable intermediary in the stablecoin market. This not only created a significant compliance cost for PPSIs but also solidified the dominance of institutions that already had deep relationships and resources dedicated to such processes. The system was designed less to ensure integrity and more to perpetuate a high-cost, high-friction model of oversight.

The cumulative effect of these requirements was to create a new and significant burden of compliance, one that proved to be a formidable barrier to entry for smaller, more agile firms. The investment in specialized compliance personnel, the expenditure on external auditors and legal counsel, and the operational overhead of compiling and verifying data all served to divert resources away from product development and innovation. The high fixed costs of establishing and maintaining this compliance infrastructure ensured that the stablecoin market would remain the exclusive domain of a handful of well-capitalized institutions, thereby stifling competition and limiting the diversity of offerings.

Ultimately, this chapter will argue that the Genius Act's reporting and auditing framework, while well-intentioned, was a spectacular failure of regulatory design. It was a system that mistook bureaucracy for transparency and human-based attestation for cryptographic truth. By embedding a legacy, off-chain system of oversight into a digital-native market, the Act ensured that the most valuable and innovative stablecoin use cases—those that relied on real-time, on-chain transparency and programmatic verifiability—would inevitably migrate to platforms and jurisdictions where such antiquated rules did not apply.

Foundations of Transparency: Why Report and Disclose?

The Genius Act's reporting and disclosure requirements were born from a need to restore and build public trust in a market marred by past failures and a historical lack of transparency. Proponents of the Act argued that by mandating frequent disclosures and independent audits, the framework would ensure that stablecoin users could confidently understand the true backing and operational integrity of their assets. This was a direct attempt to combat the misinformation and fraud that had become rampant in the unregulated market. Yet, this approach was a spectacular failure of imagination. Instead of leveraging the cryptographic certainty of a distributed ledger, which could provide real-time, irrefutable proof of reserves, the Act chose to rely on a legacy system of periodic, human-intensive reporting that was fundamentally time-delayed and costly.

These reporting mechanisms were also positioned as a vital tool for regulatory oversight and risk monitoring. The Act's framers intended to give regulators the ability to assess an issuer's solvency, monitor for compliance, and identify potential systemic risks in real-time. This information was meant to inform policy decisions and guide future regulatory adjustments. However, the reliance on monthly attestations and quarterly filings meant that regulators were perpetually looking in the rearview mirror. In a digital market where events can unfold in minutes, a monthly report is a historical artifact, not a tool for real-time risk management. The system, therefore, created a false sense of security, providing regulators with a mountain of data that was already outdated by the time it was received and processed.

Finally, the reporting requirements were intended to facilitate market integrity and confidence by providing reliable, verifiable data for market participants and analysts. By promoting fair competition based on verifiable claims, the Act aimed to enhance the credibility of U.S.-issued stablecoins on the global stage. While this goal was laudable, the method was flawed. The high cost of compliance and the complexity of the reporting process became a significant barrier to entry, ensuring that only a handful of well-resourced entities could participate. Instead of fostering a competitive market, the framework created an oligopoly where competition was based not on technological superiority or innovation, but on a firm's ability to navigate a bureaucratic labyrinth.

Detailed Reporting and Disclosure Requirements

The Genius Act's specific requirements for mandatory monthly public disclosures of reserve composition were a central pillar of its transparency framework. Issuers were required to provide a detailed breakdown of their reserve assets, including the specific maturities of U.S. Treasury securities and the amounts held in U.S. currency. This information was to be made easily accessible to the public, typically on the PPSI's website. However, this periodic disclosure, while a step up from the previous unregulated market, was a poor substitute for the real-time, on-chain proof of reserves that was already technologically feasible. By relying on a monthly attestation, the system created a thirty-day window of vulnerability where a stablecoin's reserves could be, in theory, mismanaged or manipulated without immediate public knowledge.

Issuers were also required to have publicly available redemption policies and fee structures. The Act mandated that PPSIs provide clear and conspicuous procedures for stablecoin redemption at par, along with a full disclosure of all associated fees. This was intended to ensure that users had predictable and transparent access to the underlying fiat currency. While this provision was a necessary consumer protection, it also had the effect of locking issuers into a rigid business model. The requirement to publish and adhere to a fixed fee structure reduced a PPSI's ability to adapt to changing market conditions or to introduce innovative, tiered service offerings.

The most extensive requirements were the quarterly and annual regulatory filings. These went far beyond reserve composition, demanding comprehensive financial statements, operational reports, and granular data on transaction volumes and customer demographics. This was an attempt to provide primary regulators with a full picture of the PPSI's health, but it created an enormous bureaucratic burden. These extensive filings, often requiring specific data formats and secure submission channels, were a massive undertaking that diverted significant time and resources from a firm's core business of stablecoin issuance. This was a classic case of regulatory overreach, demanding an excessive amount of data that was both costly to compile and of questionable utility for real-time risk assessment.

The Critical Role of Independent Audits

A cornerstone of the Genius Act was the reliance on monthly third-party attestations of reserve reports. This mandate required that only Public Company Accounting Oversight Board (PCAOB) registered accounting firms could perform these attestations, which were meant to verify the accuracy of the reserve composition and valuation. While the goal was to ensure integrity and prevent conflicts of interest, the result was the institutionalization of a costly and time-delayed intermediary. This was an endorsement of a legacy auditing model over the cryptographic integrity of the blockchain, creating a new and profitable revenue stream for a handful of large accounting firms while simultaneously adding a significant fixed cost to the PPSI business model.

For larger issuers that met a specific threshold (e.g., $50 billion in outstanding stablecoins), the Act imposed the additional requirement of annual audited financial statements. These audits, mirroring the requirements of a publicly traded company, demanded a full assessment of balance sheets, income statements, and cash flows. This enhanced scrutiny for "systemically important" stablecoin issuers was an attempt to mitigate contagion risk. However, it also cemented the idea that a stablecoin issuer was a traditional financial firm, not a technological platform. The application of such a cumbersome and costly process to a digital asset issuer was a clear signal that the Genius Act was more concerned with fitting new technology into old boxes than with creating a new, appropriate framework.

The Act's oversight also extended to internal control audits and operational reviews, including assessments of cybersecurity and anti-money laundering (AML) protocols. These reviews were intended to ensure the robustness of the technological infrastructure supporting stablecoin issuance. While cybersecurity and operational resilience were critical concerns, the Genius Act's approach was to impose a top-down, checklist-driven auditing process. This approach was far less effective than a system that could programmatically and immutably enforce these controls on-chain, and it once again created a significant compliance burden that favored large, established institutions over agile, technologically-driven startups.

This fundamental element of the Genius Act fails on one of the key areas of cryptocurrency attestation, the need for security and code audit. These audits show the reliability of the code for the project. Furthermore, it is imperative to note that there is a need for advanced assessment methods, such the Government Blockchain Association's Blockchain Maturity Model, approved by the United Nations, or even something as simple as ISO 20022. However, the Genius Act failed to explore either of the avenues for development.

Scalability Challenges and the Burden of Compliance

The most significant and predictable consequence of the Genius Act's oversight framework was the significant compliance costs for PPSIs. The investment in specialized legal and compliance personnel, the expenditure on sophisticated technology solutions for data collection and reporting, and the ongoing fees for external auditors and legal counsel created a massive, fixed-cost overhead. This was an economic drag on the entire system, one that served no purpose other than to satisfy a time-delayed, off-chain regulatory process. The burden of these costs was a direct impediment to profitability and scalability for any firm seeking to enter the market.

This compliance burden created an enormous amount of operational overhead and resource diversion. Management and staff were required to spend an inordinate amount of time on data compilation and verification, tasks that were repetitive, costly, and non-value-adding. This focus on compliance inevitably led to slower product development cycles, as engineering and product teams were forced to dedicate resources to satisfying regulatory requirements instead of building new, innovative features. The Genius Act's framework, in its single-minded pursuit of safety, effectively eliminated the agility and responsiveness that had been the hallmarks of a rapidly evolving digital market.

These high fixed costs and operational overhead were a powerful disincentive for new entrants and smaller issuers. The barrier to entry was so high that it effectively insulated the market from the kind of competitive pressure that drives innovation. This created a stagnant ecosystem where a few large, well-resourced incumbent financial institutions had a monopoly on stablecoin issuance. By limiting competition and diversity, the Genius Act ultimately undermined its own stated goal of creating a robust and healthy U.S. stablecoin market.

Finally, the framework was buttressed by the threat of severe penalties for non-compliance and reputational risk. The Act included provisions for significant civil and criminal penalties for false certifications or other violations. This created a culture of fear and extreme risk aversion among PPSIs, leading them to be overly conservative in their business practices. The risk of enforcement actions, coupled with the potential for irreparable reputational damage, ensured that PPSIs would never push the boundaries of innovation. They became, by design, sterile and static entities, while the true innovation continued to flourish in the unregulated shadows of the global market.

Conclusion

The reporting, disclosure, and audit requirements of the Genius Act, as detailed in this chapter, were a regulatory paradox. Conceived as a way to build trust and prevent fraud, they instead became a source of economic inefficiency, a barrier to entry, and a powerful disincentive for innovation. By clinging to the legacy methods of traditional finance, the Act's framers failed to grasp the transformative potential of a distributed ledger for providing transparency in a new, more robust way. The result was a system that provided the illusion of oversight while the true, on-chain revolution was happening beyond its purview.

The reliance on periodic, off-chain attestations and audits, while a familiar comfort to regulators, was a significant step backward from what was technically possible. In a market where transactions are immutable and publicly verifiable, the Act chose to prioritize time-delayed, costly, and human-intensive oversight. This created an audit-and-report industry that extracted significant value without providing a commensurate increase in security or trust. The economic cost of this inefficiency was immense, diverting capital and talent that could have been used to build more secure, transparent, and scalable solutions native to the digital asset ecosystem.

The compliance burden created by the Genius Act was not a bug, but a feature. The significant costs associated with specialized personnel, external auditors, and legal counsel were a formidable hurdle for any firm not already operating with deep pockets and a pre-existing compliance department. This had the predictable effect of consolidating the market, ensuring that the PPSI ecosystem would remain an oligopoly of a few large, incumbent financial institutions. By design, the Genius Act effectively priced out the very fintech startups and crypto-native firms that were poised to drive innovation, limiting market dynamism and entrenching the status quo.

Furthermore, the Act's emphasis on periodic reporting and auditing was a dangerous form of regulatory theater. While the public received monthly disclosures, the underlying technology had the potential for real-time, on-chain verification of reserves and transactions. The Genius Act's framers, in their conservative approach, chose to ignore this possibility, creating a system that was always one step behind the market. This made it a poor tool for real-time risk management and a powerful incentive for market participants to seek a more transparent, verifiable, and ultimately more trustworthy system built on the immutable logic of the blockchain itself.

In conclusion, the Genius Act's reporting, disclosure, and auditing provisions were not a success. They were a regulatory failure that revealed a profound lack of understanding of the technology they sought to govern. By imposing an antiquated framework on a forward-looking industry, the Act created a market that was safe but sterile, transparent but time-delayed, and compliant but costly. This regulatory overreach, in its single-minded pursuit of a traditional model of trust, ironically created a powerful impetus for a market shift toward new forms of decentralized, cryptographically verifiable assets—the very Asset-Backed Tokens (ABTs) that were being forged in the global regulatory vacuum left by the Genius Act's myopic vision.

Chapter 4: Strict Limitation on Permissible activities for issuers

“We are quickly approaching the stage of ultimate inversion: the stage where the government is free to do anything it pleases, while the citizens may act only by permission; which is the stage of the darkest periods of human history, the stage of rule by brute force.”

Ayn Rand[7]

The Genius Act, in its overarching quest for stability, was defined not only by what it required of Permitted Payment Stablecoin Issuers (PPSIs), but also by what it explicitly forbade. The legislation’s most significant and consequential set of provisions were the strict limitations on permissible activities, which codified a "payment only" mandate. This chapter will argue that while this narrow scope was ostensibly intended to focus stablecoins on their role as a safe and stable medium of exchange, it was in reality a fatal miscalculation. By stripping stablecoins of their ability to be productive and by insulating them from the broader digital asset ecosystem, the Genius Act rendered the PPSI framework economically sterile and technologically irrelevant, setting the stage for a new class of assets that would flourish in the regulatory void.

---

[7] Staff (2025). “Permission Quotes.” Brainy Quote at https://www.brainyquote.com/topics/permission-quotes.

The core of the "payment only" mandate defined a PPSI's role with surgical precision: the issuance and redemption of payment stablecoins, the management of required reserves, and the provision of related custodial services. This narrow scope was intended to prevent "mission creep" into traditional banking or investment activities, thereby insulating stablecoins from the broader financial risks that had plagued traditional markets. The Act's framers believed that by keeping stablecoins simple, they could keep them safe. This belief, however, was predicated on an outdated understanding of digital assets, which derive their value not from their static nature but from their dynamic utility within a programmable, on-chain environment.

The legislative mindset was most vividly demonstrated by the explicit exclusion of yield-bearing activities. This provision, as we have already explored, was a direct and forceful move to distinguish stablecoins from interest-bearing deposits or securities. It was a pre-emptive strike against the perceived threat of "shadow banking" and unbacked lending. Yet, by making it illegal to pay a yield to a stablecoin holder, the Genius Act created an asset class with a fundamental economic flaw. In a decentralized ecosystem where capital is expected to be productive, a non-yielding asset is an economically inferior one. This single rule was the primary disincentive for institutional adoption and on-chain integration.

The Genius Act also included a series of powerful prohibitions, borrowed directly from legacy financial regulation. The "tying" prohibition, for instance, barred PPSIs from conditioning stablecoin services on the purchase of other products. This was an attempt to prevent large tech companies or financial conglomerates from leveraging their market power, a valid concern in traditional commerce. However, its application to the digital economy, where seamless integration and bundled services are often a feature, was a regressive step. It created an isolated and fractured user experience, hindering the very innovations that could have made stablecoins a mainstream payment method.

The Act's philosophy of control was further underscored by its adherence to the long-standing U.S. policy of separating banking and commerce. By imposing a general prohibition on non-financial public companies from issuing stablecoins, the Act sought to prevent potential conflicts of interest and excessive economic concentration. While this may have been prudent for an era of industrial conglomerates, its application to the digital world was a significant hurdle. It prevented the very entities best positioned to drive stablecoin adoption—large tech platforms and commercial enterprises—from participating, thus ensuring that stablecoins would remain a niche product within a walled-off financial garden.

These limitations had a cascading effect, forcing PPSIs to adopt constrained and often unviable business models. Without the ability to generate revenue from interest on reserves, issuers were forced to shift to a transaction-fee-based model, which presented significant challenges for profitability and scalability. This constrained business model discouraged investment in infrastructure and innovation, and it made PPSIs a fundamentally unattractive proposition for venture capital and strategic partnerships. The result was a market that was stagnant, uncompetitive, and increasingly isolated from the more dynamic global digital asset economy.

Ultimately, the limitations on permissible activities were the defining feature of the PPSI framework's failure. They ensured that PPSIs would remain primarily a "bridge" for crypto trading rather than a common consumer payment method, hindering the seamless, integrated digital finance experiences that the technology promised. This chapter will demonstrate how this regulatory overreach, by creating a sterile and economically unviable asset class, became a powerful and unwitting catalyst for the rise of Asset-Backed Tokens (ABTs)—digital assets that offered both productivity and security, but did so entirely outside the purview of the Genius Act.

Defining the Scope: The "Payment Only" Mandate

The Genius Act's core definition of a Permitted Payment Stablecoin Issuer (PPSI) was deliberately restrictive, with its mandate for core permitted activities narrowly focused on the functions of a simple payment mechanism. This included the issuance and redemption of payment stablecoins, the passive management of the required 1:1 reserves, and the provision of related custodial services. The Act also allowed for other activities "directly supporting" these core functions, a vague clause that would become a source of regulatory friction and uncertainty. By defining the scope so narrowly, the Act's framers ensured that PPSIs would be little more than digital money changers, a role that was fundamentally at odds with the programmable and composable nature of assets in the broader digital ecosystem.

The intent behind this narrow scope was to keep stablecoins focused on their role as a means of payment and settlement, thereby preventing "mission creep" into traditional banking or investment activities. Regulators sought to limit exposure to broader financial risks, believing that a static, non-productive asset was the safest asset. This was a classic case of fighting the last war. The framers' worldview was shaped by the risks of fractional-reserve banking and speculative investment, and they applied this lens to a technology that was, by its very design, capable of cryptographic proof and real-time transparency. In their effort to make stablecoins safe, they made them sterile, ignoring that their true value lies in their utility within an integrated, dynamic ecosystem.

The most profound economic and technological consequence of this narrow scope was the explicit exclusion of yield-bearing activities. This provision was a direct effort to reinforce the non-interest-bearing nature of payment stablecoins and distinguish them from deposits or securities. It was intended to prevent the creation of a "shadow banking" system through stablecoin lending. However, this absolute prohibition was a fatal flaw. It eliminated the primary economic incentive for holding a stablecoin beyond a brief transactional window. In doing so, the Genius Act ensured that compliant stablecoins would be economically inferior to other digital assets and financial instruments, creating a powerful disincentive for institutional adoption and on-chain integration.

Prohibitions: Preventing Unfair Practices and Systemic Risks

The Genius Act's prohibition on "tying" was an attempt to import a legacy anti-competitive concern into the digital market. The Act barred PPSIs from conditioning stablecoin services on the purchase of other products, with the intention of preventing large tech companies or financial conglomerates from leveraging their market power to dominate the stablecoin ecosystem. This provision, while a familiar tool in antitrust law, was a significant impediment to innovation in the digital economy. It created an artificial separation between payments and other services, hindering the development of seamless, integrated user experiences that are a hallmark of modern technology platforms.

The Act's firm adherence to the long-standing U.S. policy of the separation of banking and commerce was another example of its reliance on outdated regulatory models. The policy was designed to prevent conflicts of interest and excessive economic concentration by stopping large commercial firms from dominating the financial system. However, in the context of stablecoins, this provision became a major obstacle to adoption. It prevented the very entities that had the user bases and technological expertise to drive widespread adoption—large commercial and tech firms—from becoming issuers. This ensured that the stablecoin would remain a niche financial product, rather than a mainstream payment and settlement vehicle integrated into everyday life.

The restrictions on non-financial public companies were a further refinement of this isolationist philosophy. The Genius Act placed a general prohibition on such entities from issuing stablecoins, with the possibility of an exception only through the unanimous approval of the Stablecoin Certification Review Committee (SCRC). The specific rules regarding data usage by such approved entities, to protect consumer privacy, created yet another layer of compliance. This provision, in its zealous pursuit of a controlled, siloed financial system, guaranteed that the most well-resourced and technologically capable firms would either not participate or would be bogged down in a lengthy and uncertain regulatory process.

Consequences of Permissible Activity Limitations

The strict limitations on permissible activities had a devastating impact on stablecoin business models. With the profitable revenue stream of yield on reserves eliminated, issuers were forced to pivot to a model based on transaction fees or other related services. This created significant challenges for profitability and scalability, as a fee-based model is far more difficult to scale than one built on passive interest income. This forced pivot discouraged investment in infrastructure and innovation, and it made the PPSI a fundamentally unattractive proposition for venture capital and strategic partnerships, leading to a stagnant and uncompetitive market.

These limitations were also a powerful force for constraining innovation and ecosystem development. By isolating PPSIs from the broader digital asset ecosystem, the Act actively discouraged the development of new, novel use cases beyond simple payments. This prevented the seamless integration of stablecoins into "Web3" applications and stifled the emergence of multi-functional stablecoin platforms. The Genius Act's framework effectively put a technological and economic moat around the PPSI, ensuring it would remain a sterile and isolated asset, disconnected from the very ecosystem it was meant to serve.

The limitations had a direct and negative implication for user experience and utility. Because PPSIs were non-yielding and disconnected from the broader digital ecosystem, they remained primarily a "bridge" for crypto trading, rather than a common consumer payment method. Users who sought a more seamless, integrated digital finance experience—one that blended payments with other services and offered a return on their capital—were forced to look for stablecoin alternatives in jurisdictions with broader permissible activities. The Genius Act, in its attempt to create a perfect payment stablecoin, inadvertently ensured it would be a stablecoin that nobody wanted to use for payment.

Navigating the Boundaries: Compliance and Future Evolution

For a PPSI, navigating the Genius Act was a complex and ongoing challenge, particularly due to the ambiguity surrounding regulatory guidance. The Act's reliance on vague phrases such as "directly supporting" a core function left the door open for subjective interpretation and regulatory guidance from regulators. This created a climate of uncertainty, where PPSIs had to constantly seek clarity to prevent inadvertent non-compliance. This need for clear guidance was a testament to the Act's poor design, which prioritized broad, unspecific rules over the kind of clear, programmatic requirements that are best suited for the digital age.

In this restrictive environment, strategic adaptation for PPSIs became a matter of survival. Issuers were forced to focus on building core payment infrastructure and forming partnerships within the narrow, regulated sandbox they were given. They had to develop value-added services around stablecoin issuance without crossing the legal lines, and explore opportunities within the defined boundaries, such as identity or data services for payments. This was not a recipe for innovation, but a strategy for risk-aversion, ensuring that PPSIs would be slow-moving, bureaucratic entities rather than agile, market-leading platforms.

Finally, the inherent flaws of the Genius Act created a constant conversation around the potential for future legislative adjustments. As the stablecoin market evolved and new use cases emerged in other jurisdictions, the U.S. framework became increasingly isolated and outdated. The debate became one of balancing regulatory prudence with the need for innovation, and the Act's failure was an increasingly powerful argument for legislative reform. The international comparisons, which consistently showed more dynamic and competitive markets emerging elsewhere, provided an undeniable influence on U.S. policy in the long term, ultimately proving that a myopic focus on stability can be the greatest source of instability.

Conclusion

The Genius Act's strict limitations on the permissible activities of a PPSI were the most profound and ultimately self-defeating aspect of the legislation. While they were meticulously designed to ensure a stablecoin's safety and focus on a "payment only" function, they were a complete failure in practice. By creating a static, non-productive asset and a rigid, isolated ecosystem, the Act's framers inadvertently guaranteed the marginalization of the very stablecoins they were trying to protect. The net effect was a regulatory framework that was perfectly safe, perfectly compliant, and perfectly irrelevant to the broader trajectory of digital finance.

The most damaging of these limitations was the explicit prohibition of yield-bearing activities. This rule was not just a technical requirement; it was an ideological statement that revealed a profound misunderstanding of the digital economy. It treated a stablecoin as a simple digital substitute for a physical dollar, rather than as a programmable, composable asset that could be a foundational building block for new forms of financial activity. In a market where capital is expected to be productive, the Genius Act created a digital equivalent of a vault, an asset that was designed to be held but not used, and in doing so, it ensured that PPSIs would never be able to compete with more dynamic alternatives.

The prohibitions against "tying" and the separation of banking and commerce, while derived from sound principles of legacy finance, were equally destructive. They prevented a robust, integrated ecosystem from forming around PPSIs, ensuring that they would remain isolated and uncompetitive. The Act's insistence on a siloed model of financial services was a direct contradiction of the "Web3" ethos, which is built on the seamless integration of payments, identity, data, and other services. By enforcing a dated regulatory model, the Genius Act created a fractured user experience and a powerful incentive for both users and developers to seek out platforms and assets that were built for a more integrated future.

The Genius Act, therefore, didn't just fail to foster innovation; it actively created the conditions for a regulatory arbitrage. The constrained PPSI market, with its limited activities and non-yielding assets, was a powerful catalyst for capital and talent to migrate to alternative jurisdictions and asset classes. The market, in its eternal search for efficiency and utility, simply bypassed the PPSI framework entirely. This regulatory overreach, by creating an artificial and sterile environment, was the primary driver of a market evolution that was neither foreseen nor desired by the Act's framers.

In conclusion, the Genius Act's myopic focus on a "payment only" mandate was the single greatest factor in its failure. By stripping the stablecoin of its utility and its economic viability within the decentralized ecosystem, the Act inadvertently created the perfect conditions for a new, more resilient form of digital asset to emerge. As we will see, this flight from regulated stability to decentralized productivity ultimately led to the rapid and decisive rise of Asset-Backed Tokens (ABTs)—assets that solved the very problems the Genius Act created, but did so in a way that was entirely outside the purview of its outdated and flawed regulatory framework.

Chapter 5: Three Year Market Sunset for Non-Compliant Tokens and Enforcement against Digital Asset Service Providers

"The sky takes on shades of orange during sunrise and sunset, the color that gives you hope that the sun will set only to rise again."

Nathan Philips[8]

Of all the provisions within the Genius Act, none was more punitive, more controversial, or more revealing of the legislation's true intent than the three-year secondary market sunset clause. This provision was the ultimate tool of enforcement, designed not to gently guide the market toward compliance, but to surgically excise any digital asset that did not conform to the Act's rigid Permitted Payment Stablecoin Issuer (PPSI) framework. It was a legislative blunt instrument that declared war on the existing stablecoin ecosystem, creating a forced market liquidation event and a legal battleground over constitutional principles. This chapter will argue that the sunset clause was not a measured regulatory tool, but a delayed ex post facto system, punishing past, legal behavior by

[8] Staff (2025). "Sunset Quotes." Brainy Quote at https://www.brainyquote.com/topics/sunset-quotes?gad_source=1&gad_campaignid=20728013932&gclid=Cj0KCQjwhafEBhCcARIsAEGZEKJ1DP96BbeY-xlxg9wNKajHWhgy4BEULAHHAQQezEtyap5-aWASDM8aAmwPEALw_wcB.

revoking the future utility of previously acquired assets.

The mechanics of the sunset provision were deceptively simple. The Act defined a "noncompliant token" as any stablecoin that was not issued by a qualified PPSI. It then granted a three-year grace period from the law's enactment. After this period expired, it became a clear and explicit prohibition for all Digital Asset Service Providers (DASPs), including exchanges, custodians, and brokers, to offer, sell, or facilitate the trading of these noncompliant tokens to U.S. persons. The effect was immediate and profound: it placed a ticking clock on the entire pre-existing stablecoin market, forcing a reckoning that was both economic and existential.

On the surface, the regulatory rationale was presented as a noble endeavor. The sunset clause was framed as a necessary measure to protect U.S. consumers from unbacked or weakly regulated stablecoins. Proponents of the Act argued that it was essential to remove perceived financial stability risks from the U.S. system and to ensure a clear, well-regulated market for payment stablecoins. This narrative, however, glossed over the clause's true nature. It was not merely about future stability; it was about forcing compliance by making noncompliance an economic impossibility. It was a top-down, centralized attempt to re-engineer an entire market from scratch.

Beneath this regulatory veneer lay the core legal challenge that would dominate the conversation: the potential for the sunset clause to be a violation of the Ex Post Facto Clause of the U.S. Constitution. While this clause traditionally applies to criminal law, its underlying principle—that a person cannot be punished for an act that was legal at the time it was committed—has broader applications in civil and economic regulation. The argument against the sunset clause was that it punished the past, legal acquisition of a stablecoin by retroactively depriving that asset of its liquidity and utility. The three-year grace period, rather than a mitigating factor, was seen by many as simply a delayed mechanism for a legal taking, a slow-motion seizure of value.

The practical implications of this provision were a source of deep market disruption. The looming deadline created an imperative for DASPs to begin delisting noncompliant stablecoins, leading to the risk of forced liquidation and significant illiquidity. As the sunset date approached, the value of these tokens would be driven down by market pressure, potentially leading to substantial losses for investors who had acquired them in good faith. This was not a theoretical risk but a very real and predictable consequence of a law that prioritized regulatory control over the rights of asset holders.

Ultimately, the three-year sunset clause was the Genius Act's most aggressive move, a clear signal that the U.S. was willing to break with a decentralized, free-market approach to digital assets. This chapter will explore the legal arguments for and against the clause, detail the profound market disruption it caused, and analyze the long-term consequences of such a powerful regulatory maneuver. It will argue that this attempt to control the market was not only legally fraught but ultimately counterproductive, serving as the primary catalyst for the market's migration to a new, more resilient form of digital asset.

The Three-Year Secondary Market Sunset Clause: Design and Intent

The Genius Act's three-year sunset provision was a carefully crafted mechanism designed to force a market-wide transition away from existing stablecoins. The mechanics of the clause were straightforward: it first defined a "noncompliant token" as any stablecoin that did not meet the rigorous PPSI standards. From the moment the Act was signed into law, a three-year countdown began. Once this grace period elapsed, it became explicitly illegal for any Digital Asset Service Provider (DASP)—a category that included exchanges, custodians, and brokers—to facilitate the offering, sale, or trading of these noncompliant tokens to U.S. persons. This placed a hard and unavoidable deadline on the entire stablecoin market, effectively outlawing any methodology other than the one prescribed by the Genius Act.

The regulatory rationale and objectives behind this provision were articulated as a necessary measure for public welfare and financial stability. Proponents argued that the clause was essential for forcing existing stablecoins into compliance with the new U.S. standards, thereby removing perceived systemic risks from the financial system. It was framed as a protective measure to ensure a clear and regulated market, shielding consumers from the dangers of unbacked or weakly regulated stablecoins. However, this narrative served to mask the clause's true purpose: it was a heavy-handed, anticompetitive maneuver designed to eliminate all market competition and secure the dominance of a few large, incumbent institutions that could meet the PPSI criteria.

The scope and affected entities of the sunset clause were vast and far-reaching, encompassing not just stablecoin issuers but the entire digital asset ecosystem. It had an immediate and profound impact on stablecoin projects currently operating in the U.S. market, forcing them to either undergo the costly and complex process of becoming a PPSI or face extinction within three years. The most significant consequence fell on exchanges, brokers, and custodians, which were compelled to prepare for a forced delisting of noncompliant tokens. Finally, the provision had direct implications for every U.S. person who held or transacted with a stablecoin that would become noncompliant, placing their assets on a ticking clock with an uncertain future.

The *Ex Post Facto* Challenge: Legal and Constitutional Arguments

The sunset clause's most significant legal challenge was its potential to be an unconstitutional Ex Post Facto law. In U.S. constitutional law, the Ex Post Facto Clause (Article I, Sections 9 and 10) prohibits the retroactive application of a law that punishes past conduct. While its strict application is limited to criminal law, the underlying principle—that an individual cannot be penalized for an act that was legal at the time it was committed—has a broader philosophical weight in civil and economic regulation. Key judicial tests distinguish between laws that are purely regulatory and those with a punitive effect, particularly when they retroactively change the legal consequences of past actions.

The argument for applying Ex Post Facto to the sunset clause was that it had a clear punitive effect. It deprived individuals of their property rights by revoking the usability and liquidity of assets they had legally acquired years prior. The clause's "retroactive" nature was evident in its impact on existing, not just future, stablecoins. Issuers and token holders who had engaged in perfectly legal activities before the Genius Act's enactment now faced a future where their assets would become worthless on a regulated U.S. platform. This was framed as a direct change in the legal consequences of past actions, a penalty in the form of a forced economic liquidation.

The counterarguments and regulatory defense centered on the claim that the law was not punitive but purely regulatory, aimed at the public welfare and financial stability. The government would likely argue that the law's focus was on the future conduct of DASPs—prohibiting them from offering or selling noncompliant tokens after the deadline—and not on the past conduct of token holders. This argument draws an analogy to other regulated industries where products, such as certain chemicals or older vehicle models, are later deemed non-compliant and restricted from future sale. The three-year grace period was presented as a mitigating factor, demonstrating a non-punitive intent and providing ample time for a smooth market transition.

Market Disruption and Negative Scalability

The sunset clause created an inevitable and destructive market dynamic, leading to forced delisting and liquidation risks. As the three-year deadline loomed, DASPs were legally obligated to begin delisting noncompliant stablecoins from their U.S. platforms. This created a powerful and predictable incentive for a market-wide sell-off. The resulting pressure on noncompliant tokens led to significant price volatility and illiquidity, as market participants rushed to exit their positions. This forced liquidation event had a direct and negative impact on investors and users who had acquired these tokens in good faith, potentially leading to widespread and significant losses.

Perhaps the most significant unintended consequence was the migration of activity and "stablecoin flight." Confronted with the impending ban, U.S. persons and institutions began seeking offshore avenues and platforms to continue their stablecoin transactions. This led to a surge in the use of decentralized exchanges and peer-to-peer protocols, which operate beyond the reach of U.S. regulatory oversight. The Genius Act, in its attempt to consolidate the market under its control, ironically pushed a substantial amount of stablecoin innovation and liquidity out of the U.S. domestic market and into a less-transparent, less-regulated global ecosystem.

The sunset clause presented a nearly insurmountable challenge for issuers and ecosystems. The significant financial burden and cost of achieving PPSI status within a three-year window was a barrier that only the most well-capitalized firms could overcome. This led to the fragmentation of the global stablecoin market, creating a clear and hostile divide between compliant U.S. stablecoins and the rest of the world. The loss of network effects and interoperability for noncompliant stablecoin ecosystems within the U.S. financial landscape was a decisive blow, ensuring that the PPSI-compliant market would remain an isolated and uncompetitive island.

Legal Precedent and Future Implications

The legal challenges to the sunset clause were set to rely on relevant legal precedents and analogies from other areas of regulatory law. Case law concerning the retroactive application of economic and safety regulations, particularly in fields like environmental and public health, would be central to the debate. The distinction between a "vested right" to continue a business model and a "privilege" granted by evolving regulation would be key. Ultimately, any court would be tasked with interpreting the Supreme Court's precedents on due process and the takings clause in relation to retroactive economic legislation, a complex and evolving area of law.

Given the contentious nature of the sunset clause, the likelihood of judicial review and potential litigation was extremely high. Plaintiffs were expected to launch legal challenges on both Ex Post Facto and due process grounds, arguing that the law was an arbitrary deprivation of property. The government, in turn, would defend the law on the basis of a rational basis for public interest and financial stability. The courts would play a crucial role in interpreting the precise scope of Congressional regulatory power over digital assets, and their decisions would have a profound and lasting impact on the future of the entire industry.

The sunset clause embodied the inherent policy trade-offs and unintended consequences of the Genius Act. It perfectly highlighted the tension between robust consumer protection and fostering market innovation. The Act's aggressive regulatory approach, while intended to create stability, ultimately carried the risk of driving innovation offshore and disincentivizing legitimate activity that did not fit the new regulatory mold. In the long term, the sunset clause was a clear signal to the world that the U.S. was willing to sacrifice its leadership in the global digital asset space for the sake of a centralized, controlled, and ultimately uncompetitive stablecoin market.

Conclusion

This chapter breaks down the most aggressive and controversial provision of the Genius Act: the three-year sunset clause. This provision, which effectively banned non-compliant stablecoins from the U.S. market, was a blunt instrument of regulatory control. It was designed to clear the market of all competitors, paving the way for a compliant oligopoly of a few large PPSI issuers. In its single-minded pursuit of a controlled and centralized stablecoin ecosystem, the Act's framers not only created a legal minefield but also profoundly misunderstood the nature of the market they were trying to shape.

The core of the legal challenge was the claim that the sunset clause was an unconstitutional ex post facto law in all but name. While the government argued that the law was purely regulatory and not punitive, the market fallout painted a different picture. The clause created a situation where a person's past, legal acquisition of an asset was retroactively given a penalty: the loss of its future utility and liquidity. The three-year grace period, while framed as a transition, was effectively a ticking time bomb, a slow-motion liquidation event that punished holders of non-compliant tokens for their prior decisions.

The economic fallout was immediate and predictable. The imperative for DASPs to delist noncompliant stablecoins created a significant risk of forced delisting and liquidation. As the sunset deadline approached, the market for these tokens became increasingly illiquid, leading to price volatility and significant losses for investors. This was a clear demonstration that the law was not a smooth regulatory transition, but a state-mandated market disruption. The government's attempt to create a safe market instead led to an event that was characterized by panic selling and a destruction of value for a wide range of market participants.

The most telling consequence of the sunset clause was its role in driving activity away from the U.S. market. Rather than bringing stablecoin transactions into a regulated fold, the Act's aggressive stance caused a significant migration of activity and "stablecoin flight." U.S. persons sought offshore avenues for their transactions, and the market saw a surge in the use of decentralized exchanges and peer-to-peer transaction platforms that were beyond the reach of U.S. regulators. This created a new, more difficult-to-regulate parallel market, a powerful and unintended consequence of a law designed to create order.

The legal arguments against the sunset clause hinged on the delicate balance between a government's right to regulate in the public interest and an individual's right to not have their property arbitrarily deprived of value. The outcome of any legal challenge would have tested the limits of Congressional power over digital assets and would have set a crucial precedent for future regulation. The Genius Act, in its legislative arrogance, forced a confrontation that was both a legal and a philosophical battle over the very nature of digital property and a free-market system.

In the long run, the sunset clause was the key factor in the Genius Act's ultimate failure to secure U.S. leadership in digital finance. By creating a hostile and punitive environment for the existing market, the Act destroyed the network effects and ecosystem development of non-compliant stablecoins. It did so in the naive belief that the market would simply migrate to the compliant PPSI framework. Instead, it created a powerful impetus for a different kind of evolution.

The ultimate irony is that the sunset clause, in its attempt to kill off all competition, became the primary catalyst for the rise of Asset-Backed Tokens (ABTs). By making existing stablecoins untenable, the Act created a market need for a new asset class that was more resilient, more decentralized, and less susceptible to the kind of arbitrary regulatory delisting that the Genius Act embodied. The sunset clause was the single most powerful and unwitting tool in driving the market to a solution that was entirely beyond the control of the U.S. regulatory framework, proving that the market, in its perpetual search for freedom and utility, will always find a way around even the most aggressive of regulatory walls.

Chapter 6: The Killing of Algos (How Smart Currency is a Threat to Fiat Hegemony)

“This is where the world is going: direct access from anywhere to any type of data, whether it’s a small pice of data or a small answer but a long algorithm to create that answer. The user does not care about this.”

Hasso Plattner[9]

The Genius Act, in its totality, was a profound and multifaceted piece of legislation, yet its most pointed and ideologically charged provisions were aimed squarely at the heart of decentralized finance: algorithmic stablecoins. This chapter will explore how the Act's carefully constructed definitions and stringent requirements served not as a broad regulatory framework, but as a deliberate and surgical strike against a specific form of digital money. This was more than an act of regulation; it was a powerful, defensive measure to protect the hegemony of fiat currency. By making it legally and technically impossible for algorithmic stablecoins to exist as "payment stablecoins" in the U.S. market, the Genius Act effectively killed this nascent innovation, eliminating a potential threat to traditional monetary control before it could fully mature.

---

[9] Staff (2025). “Algorithm Quotes.” Brainy Quote at https://www.brainyquote.com/topics/algorithm-quotes.

The first and most elegant blow against algorithmic stablecoins was delivered through the Act's very narrow definition of a "payment stablecoin." This definition, which emphasized an issuer's explicit obligation to convert, redeem, or repurchase for a fixed monetary value, was crafted with a traditional mindset. The language was deliberately exclusionary, focusing on a one-to-one, issuer-backed model. By doing so, the Act implicitly left no room for stablecoins that derived their value from code, incentives, and supply/demand dynamics without a tangible, traditional reserve backing and a legal obligation from a recognized issuer. This was a "death by definition," a pre-emptive strike that made algorithmic stablecoins non-existent as a legal entity for payment purposes in the U.S.

The second and perhaps most fatal blow came in the form of the Act’s mandatory 1:1 reserve backing and its list of permitted reserve assets. Algorithmic stablecoins, by their very design, are typically under-collateralized or uncollateralized, relying on the market capitalization of a companion asset to maintain their peg. This core design principle stands in direct and irreconcilable conflict with the Genius Act’s requirement that every payment stablecoin be backed 1:1 by traditional assets. Furthermore, the Act’s strict list of High-Quality Liquid Assets (HQLAs)—which explicitly excluded cryptocurrencies and other volatile assets—directly prevented algorithmic stablecoins, which often relied on volatile cryptocurrencies as their backing mechanism, from ever qualifying as compliant.

Beyond reserves, the Genius Act's issuer requirements sealed the fate of decentralized algorithms. The Act mandated that every payment stablecoin must have a legally identifiable issuer, a Permitted Payment Stablecoin Issuer (PPSI), which would be a regulated entity with legal obligations. Purely decentralized, algorithm-driven stablecoins, by their nature, lack a single, identifiable entity to hold accountable. This fundamental disconnect was further exacerbated by the Act's requirement for issuers to have a "kill switch" capability—the technical ability to seize, freeze, or burn stablecoins under lawful directives. This directly contradicted the core ethos of censorship resistance and immutability that animates many algorithmic designs, making compliance a technical and ideological impossibility.

Ultimately, this chapter will show that the Genius Act left no practical or legal pathway for algorithmic stablecoins to operate in the U.S. market. While the Act's framers presented this as a necessary measure for consumer protection and financial stability, the effect was to stifle a specific, capital-efficient innovation. The Act did not just ban a type of stablecoin; it also created a new class of "non-payment stablecoins" that would exist in a regulatory gray area, with their future uncertain and subject to further scrutiny. By doing so, the U.S. risked stifling a crucial avenue of innovation and pushing it offshore, cementing its focus on fiat-backed dominance at the cost of broader technological leadership.

The Definitional Strike: What is a "Payment Stablecoin"?

The Genius Act's most surgical and effective attack on algorithmic stablecoins began not with a direct ban, but with a seemingly neutral narrow definition of "payment stablecoin". The Act defined this term as a digital asset designed for payment or settlement, where the issuer is obligated to convert, redeem, or repurchase it for a fixed monetary value. This definition's emphasis on the issuer's explicit obligation for redemption at a fixed price was its crucial and most exclusionary feature. This language was deliberately crafted to fit a traditional, asset-backed model, and it left no room for assets that derived their stability from a different, less-traditional mechanism. It created a legal framework where any asset that did not have a human-run, legally accountable issuer with a direct redemption obligation could not be a payment stablecoin.

This definition, by its very design, led to the implicit exclusion of algorithmic mechanisms. Algorithmic stablecoins, by their nature, rely on code, incentives, and supply/demand dynamics to maintain their peg. They do not have a single, identifiable issuer with a legal commitment to redeem at par; rather, their stability is an emergent property of their underlying code and market arbitrage. The Genius Act's definition, which did not contemplate value stability derived solely from algorithms without a tangible, traditional reserve backing and a legal obligation from a recognized issuer, ensured that no purely algorithmic stablecoin could ever legally qualify as a payment stablecoin. This was a "death by definition," a pre-emptive strike that eliminated an entire class of digital assets from the U.S. payment system before they could be fully utilized.

Reserve Requirements: The Fatal Blow to Algorithmic Designs

The Genius Act's mandate for mandatory 1:1 reserve backing was a direct and irreconcilable conflict with the core design principles of algorithmic stablecoins. By requiring every payment stablecoin to be backed 1:1 by traditional assets, the Act outlawed any design that relied on fractional reserves or no reserves at all. Algorithmic stablecoins, by their very nature, are typically under-collateralized, relying on the market capitalization of a volatile companion asset (such as the Luna-Terra model) to maintain their peg. The Act's rigid reserve framework was therefore not just a regulatory hurdle, but a technical impossibility for any stablecoin that was not already a traditional, fiat-backed one.

This incompatibility was further cemented by the Act's strict list of Permitted Reserve Assets: only "High-Quality Liquid Assets" (HQLAs). The Act's list was intentionally narrow and included U.S. currency, demand deposits at insured institutions, short-term U.S. Treasury securities, and overnight repurchase agreements. Most importantly, it included an explicit exclusion of volatile assets, specifically banning reserves in other cryptocurrencies or commodity-backed assets. This was a direct strike against algorithmic stablecoins, which often relied on volatile cryptocurrencies as their backing collateral. This provision ensured that even if an algorithmic stablecoin could somehow manage a 1:1 backing, its underlying assets would be deemed non-compliant, making the entire project unviable.

The third pillar of the reserve framework, the prohibition on rehypothecation of reserves, was another fatal blow. The Act stipulated that reserves could not be re-used, lent out, or leveraged. This was in direct conflict with the complex lending, borrowing, and burning/minting mechanisms that are central to many algorithmic models. These designs rely on the dynamic use of collateral to maintain the peg, a practice that the Genius Act explicitly forbade. The Act's framers, in their zealous pursuit of a safe and sound stablecoin, created a regulatory environment where the most innovative and capital-efficient aspects of algorithmic stablecoins were not just discouraged, but illegal.

Issuer Requirements: No Place for Decentralized Algorithms

The Genius Act’s requirement for a "Permitted Payment Stablecoin Issuer" (PPSI) was the final nail in the coffin for decentralized algorithms. PPSIs must be a regulated legal entity, such as a bank subsidiary or a federally/state-qualified nonbank, that can be held accountable for redemption, regulatory compliance, and personal certification of reserves by its executives. This requirement is fundamentally incompatible with the decentralized, code-driven nature of algorithmic stablecoins, which intentionally lack a single, identifiable legal entity that can fulfill these stringent obligations. The Act essentially said that if a stablecoin was not run by a human-controlled, regulated institution, it could not exist as a payment stablecoin in the U.S.

This disconnect was further exacerbated by the Act's operational requirements and "kill switch" capabilities. The law mandated that issuers must demonstrate the technical capability to "seize, freeze, or burn" stablecoins under lawful directives, such as sanctions or illicit finance concerns. This requirement directly contradicts the core ethos of censorship resistance and immutability that is central to many algorithmic stablecoins. These protocols are designed to be unstoppable, to be governed by code rather than by the whims of a centralized authority. A system that is governed by a decentralized algorithm cannot realistically comply with a legal order to freeze or burn specific tokens without a centralized point of control, which would defeat the entire purpose of the design.

Market Consequences and Regulatory Future

The combined effect of these provisions was a "death by definition" for algorithmic stablecoins in the U.S.. The Genius Act left no practical or legal pathway for them to operate as payment stablecoins, effectively culling them from the U.S. market. This was a deliberate and successful outcome, rooted in the consumer protection rationale that aimed to prevent future losses from inherently volatile, unbacked, or under-collateralized designs. By eliminating this entire category of stablecoins, the Act ensured that the U.S. payment system would only use a model that was a perfect digital analog to traditional, asset-backed financial products.

While the Act was hostile to algorithmic stablecoins, it did acknowledge their existence by directing the Treasury Secretary to conduct a study of "non-payment stablecoins". This was not a sign of future acceptance, but a clear signal that any re-evaluation or future regulation of these assets would be separate from the PPSI framework and likely subject to even greater scrutiny. This provision ensured that algorithmic stablecoins would exist in a state of perpetual regulatory purgatory, with their future uncertain and their perceived risks always at the forefront of any policy discussion.

In the long term, the Genius Act's killing of algos had a profound impact on U.S. innovation and global competitiveness. By eliminating these designs from the payment stablecoin market, the U.S. sacrificed a significant opportunity to explore more capital-efficient and potentially resilient stability models. This created a powerful incentive for this type of innovation to simply move to other, less-regulated jurisdictions, potentially increasing risk for U.S. investors who might access them from abroad. The Act, in its single-minded pursuit of a traditional, fiat-backed model, cemented the U.S.'s focus on dollar dominance in the digital asset space but at the cost of excluding a diverse and innovative array of alternative stability mechanisms.

Conclusion

The Genius Act's provisions, meticulously detailed throughout this chapter, were a masterclass in legislative precision. They were a targeted and successful effort to eliminate algorithmic stablecoins from the U.S. market, not through an outright ban, but through a series of definitional, technical, and operational requirements that made them legally and practically unviable. This was a strategic move to defend fiat hegemony, a clear signal that the U.S. regulatory apparatus was unwilling to allow a form of "smart currency" that was not beholden to a centralized, human-run authority. The Genius Act didn't just regulate; it culled, ensuring that only those stablecoins that resembled traditional financial products could survive.

The first and most elegant blow was the definitional strike. By crafting a definition of a "payment stablecoin" that revolved entirely around an issuer's explicit, one-to-one redemption obligation, the Act rendered any stablecoin that relied on code and incentives for stability an immediate non-starter. This was a preemptive measure, a legal "no-fly zone" that prevented algorithmic stablecoins from even entering the conversation as a legitimate form of payment. The Act was not reacting to a specific failure; it was legislating a future where such an asset could not exist, thus eliminating a potential threat to fiat currency before it could ever take root.

This was then followed by the technical coup de grâce: the mandatory reserve requirements. Algorithmic stablecoins, which operate on the principle of capital efficiency and often rely on volatile companion assets for backing, were fundamentally incompatible with the Genius Act's demand for 1:1 reserves of traditional, "High-Quality Liquid Assets." This was a technical impossibility, a regulatory paradox that guaranteed a compliant stablecoin could not be an algorithmic stablecoin. The Act's rigid reserve framework was the ultimate physical barrier, ensuring that the very mechanics of a decentralized, algo-driven protocol would never be able to meet the standards of a centralized, bank-like system.

The ideological and operational incompatibility of the two systems was made starkly clear in the issuer requirements and "kill switch" capabilities. Algorithmic stablecoins are, at their core, a philosophical statement against central control. They are designed for immutability and censorship resistance. The Genius Act's mandate for a legally accountable PPSI with the technical ability to seize, freeze, or burn tokens was a direct contradiction of this ethos. It was a requirement that made compliance not just a technical challenge, but a philosophical betrayal. The Act effectively said to the market, "Your currency is not smart if we cannot turn it off."

The consequences of this targeted attack were immediate and far-reaching. The Genius Act created a legal framework where no practical or legal pathway existed for algorithmic stablecoins to operate in the U.S. market. While this was framed as a necessary measure for consumer protection, it was a profound act of regulatory suppression. The Act's direction for the Treasury Secretary to study "non-payment stablecoins" was not an olive branch but a clear signal that any future regulation of these assets would be met with even greater skepticism and scrutiny, further solidifying their status as a "threat."

Ultimately, the Genius Act's war on algorithmic stablecoins was a strategic success for the defenders of fiat hegemony, but a long-term failure for U.S. innovation. By eliminating this diverse design from the payment stablecoin market, the U.S. sacrificed an opportunity to foster more capital-efficient and potentially resilient stability mechanisms. The innovation that the Act sought to destroy did not simply disappear; it migrated to other, less regulated jurisdictions, where it continued to evolve outside of the U.S. domestic market. In its pursuit of control, the U.S. pushed a new form of "smart currency" into the regulatory shadows, proving that a myopic focus on one model of stability can ultimately lead to a loss of relevance and a flight of the very innovation it sought to contain.

Chapter 7: Increased Regulatory Cost and Compliance for Non-Bank Issuers

"The regulatory approach of the Food and Drug Administration and the Petent and Tradmark Office has driven up the cost of Generic Drugs."

J.D. Vance[10]

The Genius Act, in its extensive pursuit of financial stability and consumer protection, created a regulatory framework so rigorous that its most profound effect was not on the market as a whole, but on the very structure of competition within it. This chapter will argue that the Act's seemingly neutral requirements for compliance and oversight were, in fact, a powerful, anti-competitive force. The new rules placed a crushing regulatory cost on non-bank issuers, effectively acting as an attack on smaller companies and innovators. This created an insurmountable barrier to entry that favored only a few well-capitalized entities and traditional financial institutions, ensuring that the promise of a diverse and decentralized stablecoin market was never realized.

The first hurdle for any aspiring non-bank issuer was the rigorous application and approval process. The Act required a complex, time-consuming journey through federal or state regulatory bodies, demanding extensive documentation, legal expertise, and a

---

[10] Staff (2025). "Regulatory Quotes." Brainy Quote at https://www.brainyquote.com/topics/regulatory-quotes.

demonstration of financial soundness and operational integrity. For a small fintech or a crypto-native startup, this initial phase alone was prohibitively expensive and resource-intensive. It was a test of endurance and financial muscle, designed to filter out all but the largest and most well-prepared applicants, thus ensuring that the PPSI landscape was restricted from the outset.

Once approved, non-bank PPSIs were subjected to bank-like prudential regulation, a standard of oversight that was completely alien to the vast majority of digital asset firms. This included robust capital and liquidity requirements, as well as comprehensive risk management frameworks that covered everything from cybersecurity to interest rate risk. Implementing these sophisticated systems required significant investment in technology, infrastructure, and specialized personnel. This financial burden, while manageable for a large corporation, was a crippling fixed cost for a startup with limited capital, further cementing the competitive advantage of existing, well-established financial players.

The regulatory costs did not end with initial approval. The Act mandated ongoing supervisory oversight and examinations by the primary regulator. These were not perfunctory check-ins but deep dives into the issuer's financial health, risk management, and operational resilience. Preparing for and undergoing these examinations required a continuous drain on resources, consuming the time of senior management and dedicated compliance teams. For a small non-bank issuer, this constant state of regulatory scrutiny was a tax on their ability to grow, innovate, and respond to market demands, placing them at a significant disadvantage against larger, more resilient competitors.

In addition to these structural burdens, the Act piled on a host of operational costs, most notably through enhanced Anti-Money Laundering (AML) and Know-Your-Customer (KYC) obligations. Non-bank PPSIs were classified as full "financial institutions" under the Bank Secrecy Act (BSA), forcing them to invest in sophisticated blockchain analytics tools, identity verification services, and large, skilled compliance teams. This technical and personnel cost was yet another barrier, one that only large, established firms could absorb. The Act also demanded that issuers build the technical capabilities to freeze or seize stablecoins and report transaction data to law enforcement, a requirement that added a new layer of technical complexity and cost, especially for firms rooted in a decentralized ethos.

The cumulative effect of these requirements was to create a market that was primed for consolidation, a world where only a few powerful players could survive. This framework was particularly advantageous for existing, large-scale stablecoin issuers like Tether and Circle, which, due to their size and market capitalization, had a head start in building the required compliance and legal infrastructure. At the same time, the Act paradoxically created a pathway for traditional banks, which were already under a Federal Reserve charter, to issue their own stablecoins. This was seen by many as a form of de facto Central Bank Digital Currency (CBDC), a violation of the spirit of the Act's supposed anti-CBDC stance, as it allowed the central bank to extend its control into the digital realm through private-sector proxies.

This chapter will analyze how the regulatory high bar, far from being a public good, became the primary tool for market consolidation. We will demonstrate how the Genius Act systematically dismantled the potential for a competitive stablecoin ecosystem, ensuring that a handful of powerful entities and traditional banks would dominate the market. This not only stifled innovation but also revealed the true ideological underpinnings of the Act: a preference for centralized control over decentralized competition.

The High Bar for Entry: Licensing and Prudential Standards

The Genius Act established a formidable gateway for any non-bank entity aspiring to become a Permitted Payment Stablecoin Issuer (PPSI). The process was anything but a simple registration; it was a grueling, multi-stage gauntlet of federal or state regulatory approval. To even begin, an applicant had to prepare an exhaustive dossier demonstrating not only its financial health but also the competence of its management team and the integrity of its operational systems. This initial phase was designed to be a significant filter, requiring immense legal and consulting expertise to navigate the labyrinthine requirements. For a small fintech startup, this translated into an early and crippling capital expenditure, often before a single stablecoin could be issued. The sheer time and financial resources needed to clear this first hurdle ensured that only the most well-funded and resilient players could even attempt to enter the market.

Once past the application phase, non-bank PPSIs were immediately thrust into a regulatory environment that mirrored that of a traditional bank. This was a seismic shift for firms accustomed to the agile, low-overhead world of crypto. They were now subject to robust capital requirements, stringent liquidity management standards, and comprehensive risk management frameworks that had to cover everything from cybersecurity to market fluctuations. These were not mere suggestions but legally binding mandates that demanded significant investment in new infrastructure, technology, and specialized personnel. The cost of building these sophisticated systems—and the constant need to monitor and update them—created an ongoing, operational burden that was wholly incompatible with the lean business models of many digital asset firms.

The regulatory relationship for a PPSI was not a one-time event; it was a perpetual state of scrutiny.

Approved non-bank issuers were placed under continuous supervisory oversight, facing regular and deep-diving examinations from their primary regulator. These examinations weren't just about checking a few boxes; they were comprehensive reviews of the firm's financial health, risk posture, and overall compliance. Preparing for these constant examinations was a drain on resources, consuming the time and energy of senior leadership and dedicated teams. This created a permanent, non-revenue-generating cost center within the company, effectively slowing down a non-bank issuer's ability to innovate, grow, and pivot in a dynamic market.

Operationalizing Compliance: AML/KYC, Data, and Technology

The Genius Act classified non-bank PPSIs as "financial institutions" under the Bank Secrecy Act (BSA), a classification that came with a full suite of enhanced AML/KYC requirements. This was a non-negotiable compliance burden that mandated rigorous customer due diligence, real-time transaction monitoring, and sophisticated suspicious activity reporting (SAR) protocols. For non-bank entities, this meant investing heavily in expensive blockchain analytics tools and identity verification services. It also necessitated the hiring of a large, skilled compliance team capable of handling high volumes of data and alerts, a human capital cost that could easily rival the operational expenses of the entire firm itself.

The Act's demand for transparency was another significant operational and financial burden. PPSIs were required to provide frequent and detailed public disclosures, including monthly attestations of their reserve composition by independent third-party auditors. For larger issuers, this also meant annual audited financial statements. Building the internal systems to accurately collect, verify, and report this data was a monumental task. It required new technology solutions that could seamlessly integrate on-chain data with traditional financial reporting systems, all while managing the constant relationship and costs associated with external auditors. For a non-bank issuer, these disclosures were not just a requirement but a constant operational lift that diverted focus and resources from core business activities.

Perhaps the most ideologically challenging requirement for many non-bank issuers was the mandate to possess a "kill switch." The Act demanded that PPSIs demonstrate the technical capability to freeze, seize, or burn stablecoin balances under lawful directives. This was in direct opposition to the core tenets of censorship resistance and immutability that many digital asset firms were founded upon. Building these centralized control features, alongside secure data-sharing mechanisms for law enforcement, introduced a layer of technical complexity and risk that was both costly to implement and anathema to their decentralized ethos. The requirement effectively forced these innovators to compromise their foundational principles in the name of regulatory compliance.

Competitive Disadvantages and Market Consolidation

The regulations created by the Genius Act were a classic example of fixed costs creating a non-level playing field. The cost of obtaining a license, setting up an audit framework, and hiring a compliance team was a fixed, upfront expense that was the same for a small, new entrant as it was for a large, established player. For a small non-bank issuer with low transaction volume, this meant a disproportionately high compliance cost per unit of stablecoin issued. This made their business model economically unviable and put them at a severe disadvantage against large competitors that could leverage existing compliance infrastructures and economies of scale.

The significant time, capital, and personnel dedicated to regulatory compliance for non-bank issuers did not generate any new revenue or market share. Instead, these resources were completely diverted from areas that would have fueled growth, such as product innovation, marketing, and customer acquisition. This created a stifling effect on the entire ecosystem, slowing the pace of innovation and reducing the ability of non-bank issuers to respond quickly to market demands. In essence, the Act forced these firms to focus on regulatory survival over business growth, a dynamic that ultimately stunted the development of the U.S. stablecoin market.

The cumulative effect of these high barriers to entry and massive compliance costs was the undeniable consolidation of the stablecoin market. The regulatory burden acted as a powerful moat, protecting a few well-capitalized entities—specifically the legacy players with existing infrastructure and the financial wherewithal to comply—while systematically filtering out smaller, non-bank innovators. The Genius Act did not foster a competitive, diverse ecosystem; instead, it created a market where a handful of giants would dominate, cementing a highly concentrated stablecoin landscape in the U.S. and effectively quashing the very innovation it claimed to support.

Conclusion

The Genius Act's regulatory framework, as explored in this chapter, stands as a stark and undeniable example of how a legislative agenda ostensibly focused on stability and consumer protection can be leveraged to stifle competition and consolidate power. The high bar for entry, the bank-like prudential standards, and the enormous operational compliance costs were not neutral regulations; they were a deliberate and effective attack on smaller, non-bank innovators. The result was a market where a select few powerful players were given a significant, and in many cases, insurmountable, competitive advantage.

The non-level playing field created by the Act was a testament to the power of fixed costs in a regulated environment. For a small issuer, the cost of obtaining a license, hiring a compliance officer, and building a reporting framework represented a massive, fixed expense that was disproportionately high compared to their initial transaction volumes. By contrast, a large financial institution or a massive incumbent like Tether or Circle could absorb these costs with ease, leveraging existing infrastructure and economies of scale. The Act, therefore, guaranteed that the stablecoin market would not be a meritocracy of ideas, but a contest of financial endurance that only the largest entities could win.

The most damaging consequence of this regulatory burden was the diversion of resources from innovation and growth. For smaller, more agile firms, every dollar spent on a compliance audit or every hour spent on regulatory paperwork was a dollar and an hour not spent on building a better product, attracting new customers, or developing novel use cases. This created a stagnant ecosystem where innovation was a secondary concern to regulatory survival. This was a direct contradiction of the ethos of the digital asset market, which thrives on rapid iteration and agile development, and it ensured that the U.S. stablecoin market would remain a slow-moving and uncompetitive landscape.

The Genius Act's regulatory structure was particularly beneficial to the few large, existing stablecoin issuers and traditional banks. By making it impossible for new, small competitors to enter the market, the Act effectively solidified the position of firms like Tether and Circle, granting them a de facto oligopoly over the non-bank stablecoin space. Most troublingly, the Act created a regulatory loophole that allowed federally chartered banks to issue their own stablecoins. This was widely seen as a clever end-run around the Act's supposed ban on CBDCs, as it allowed the Federal Reserve, through its chartered institutions, to extend its monetary control into the digital realm without an explicit public rollout.

In conclusion, the Genius Act's regulatory framework was a masterful and effective strategy for market consolidation. It was a Trojan horse: a law presented as a public good that was, in reality, a powerful tool for suppressing competition and promoting a few powerful, centralized entities. The regulatory high bar was not a feature for consumer safety but a bug for innovation. By imposing a high-cost, bank-like model on a digital-native market, the Act systematically dismantled the promise of a diverse and decentralized financial ecosystem, proving once again that in a regulated landscape, the cost of entry is often the most powerful form of control.

Chapter 8: Regulatory Arbitrage and the Offshore Exodus

“You know that Moses was spinning like crazy in Exodus XIV through XVII when the Jewish people wanted to go bac and become slaves again because tramping through the deert was too hard.”

Joe Klein[11]

The pursuit of stable and efficient digital currencies has long been a central goal of the digital asset ecosystem. The GENIUS Act, a landmark piece of U.S. legislation, was intended to provide a comprehensive framework for this nascent industry, promising clarity and consumer protection. However, the Act's stringent requirements, while well-intentioned, may have inadvertently created the very conditions for regulatory arbitrage and a potential "offshore exodus." This chapter examines how the high costs and prescriptive nature of the GENIUS Act could compel companies and stablecoin issuers, particularly those now classified as Asset-Backed Tokens (ABTs), to seek more permissive jurisdictions.

The high cost of U.S. compliance under the GENIUS Act is a primary driver of this trend. Permitted Payment Stablecoin Issuers (PPSIs) face a gauntlet of requirements, including strict capital and liquidity standards, a mandatory 1:1 Highly Liquid Asset

[11] Staff (2025). “Exodus Quotes.” Brainy Quote at https://www.brainyquote.com/topics/exodus-quotes.

(HQLA) backing, and comprehensive monthly disclosures. These obligations are not merely a matter of good practice; they represent a significant financial burden. The legal, operational, and auditing costs associated with meeting these standards can be prohibitive for all but the largest and most established players. In a competitive global market, this cost differential creates a powerful incentive for companies to relocate to jurisdictions with more streamlined and less prescriptive regulations.

Furthermore, the GENIUS Act's restrictions on business models and innovation severely limit the potential for growth within the U.S. stablecoin market. By prohibiting yield on stablecoin holdings and excluding innovative designs like algorithmic stablecoins, the Act stifles creativity and closes off potentially lucrative business avenues. This stands in stark contrast to other global financial hubs that are embracing a more flexible approach. For entrepreneurs and developers who prioritize innovation and novel applications—especially those in the decentralized finance (DeFi) space—the U.S. becomes a less attractive place to build and operate.

The issue is compounded by the lengthy and cumbersome process required to become a PPSI. The time-consuming application and approval process, coupled with ongoing supervisory oversight, can significantly hinder a company's ability to launch products and adapt to a rapidly evolving market. In a sector where speed and agility are paramount, this regulatory inertia puts U.S. companies at a distinct disadvantage. Jurisdictions that have implemented nimble regulatory "sandboxes" or lighter licensing frameworks are better positioned to attract the innovators who value speed to market.

This dynamic leads directly to "jurisdiction shopping" as a mechanism of regulatory arbitrage. Stablecoin issuers with global ambitions may choose to incorporate and establish their operations in countries with more favorable legal frameworks. By doing so, they can issue stablecoins under less burdensome rules, even if these tokens are still widely accessible to U.S. users. This strategic move allows them to bypass the U.S. regulatory apparatus entirely, creating a paradox where U.S. citizens can still interact with these tokens, but the activity occurs outside of U.S. oversight.

The cumulative effect of these factors is a nascent offshore exodus of talent, capital, and innovation. The U.S. risks a "brain drain" of skilled blockchain developers and entrepreneurs who seek environments where their work can flourish without excessive regulatory friction. This flight of human capital, combined with a potential shift in venture capital and institutional investment to more permissive jurisdictions, could ultimately erode the U.S.'s competitive edge in the digital finance revolution, ceding its leadership role to other major economic blocs.

The Lure of Lighter Regulatory Regimes

The GENIUS Act's extensive requirements for Permitted Payment Stablecoin Issuers (PPSIs) represent a significant barrier to entry and a powerful motivator for regulatory arbitrage. These requirements mandate strict capital, liquidity, and risk management standards, compulsory 1:1 HQLA backing, rigorous monthly public disclosures, and comprehensive AML/KYC obligations. For a startup or an existing company seeking to enter the stablecoin market, these obligations translate into substantial legal, operational, and auditing costs that can be prohibitive. While these measures are designed to ensure stability and consumer protection, they also make it significantly cheaper and faster to operate in other jurisdictions with more streamlined or less prescriptive stablecoin regulations, effectively making U.S. compliance a luxury only a few can afford.

Beyond the financial cost, the Act's restrictions on business models and innovation are a major concern for the industry. The prohibition on paying yield on stablecoin holdings and the explicit exclusion of algorithmic stablecoins directly prevent the development of a wide range of innovative products. These limitations constrain the very business models that have driven growth in decentralized finance (DeFi) and other blockchain ecosystems. Entrepreneurs and developers who want to create more flexible stablecoin designs, integrated yield-bearing mechanisms, or novel applications for their tokens will inevitably look to other countries where such activities are not only permitted but often encouraged through more permissive frameworks.

A further disincentive is the sheer lack of speed and agility in the U.S. regulatory process. The path to becoming a PPSI is a lengthy and bureaucratic undertaking, with a prolonged application and approval process followed by continuous supervisory oversight. This slow pace is fundamentally at odds with the fast-moving, iterative nature of technology development. Innovators and startups, who must be agile to survive and thrive, cannot afford to wait for years for regulatory approval while the market and technology evolve around them. In contrast, jurisdictions that have established agile regulatory "sandboxes" or clear, efficient licensing frameworks offer a much faster path to market, thereby attracting the most dynamic and forward-thinking companies.

Mechanisms of Regulatory Arbitrage

One of the most direct forms of regulatory arbitrage is jurisdiction shopping by issuers. Stablecoin issuers, particularly those that operate in a decentralized manner or have global user bases, are not bound to a single country. They can strategically choose to incorporate and establish their primary operational base in jurisdictions that offer a more favorable regulatory environment. This allows them to issue stablecoins under a less burdensome legal and compliance framework. While their tokens may still be accessible to U.S. users, the entire issuance and operational process falls outside of U.S. regulatory purview, effectively circumventing the GENIUS Act.

Another mechanism is the shift of trading and liquidity to offshore platforms. If U.S.-regulated Digital Asset Service Providers (DASPs) are restricted from listing or trading certain stablecoins—due to the sunset clause for existing stablecoins or because a new token does not meet the Act's requirements—U.S. users will seek out alternative venues. This will lead to a migration of users and trading volume to offshore, unregulated, or less-regulated exchanges. The result is a vibrant "shadow market" for stablecoin trading that operates completely outside the oversight of U.S. authorities. This not only undermines the Act's goal of bringing digital asset activity onshore but also exposes U.S. citizens to the risks of opaque and potentially fraudulent platforms.

Clever financial engineering is also likely to emerge as a way to circumvent U.S. rules. Entities based offshore could issue "wrapped" tokens, which are digital representations of stablecoins issued in other jurisdictions. These tokens would allow U.S. users to gain indirect access to non-compliant stablecoins without technically violating the letter of the law. For example, an offshore platform might accept U.S. dollars and issue a wrapped version of a non-PPS-issued stablecoin, which could then be used in the U.S. DeFi ecosystem. This creative approach allows the market to find a way around restrictive regulations, further complicating the enforcement efforts of U.S. regulators.

The Offshore Exodus: Talent, Capital, and Innovation Flight

The U.S. faces a significant risk of a "brain drain" of crypto talent as a result of the GENIUS Act. Highly skilled blockchain developers, fintech entrepreneurs, and other crypto innovators are drawn to environments where their work is not only tolerated but actively supported. If the U.S. regulatory environment is perceived as stifling and innovation-averse, these talented individuals will naturally choose to leave the country or establish their ventures elsewhere. This loss of human capital is a direct threat to the U.S.'s long-term ability to lead in the digital asset space and will have lasting repercussions on its technological competitiveness.

This flight of talent is invariably followed by capital flight and reduced investment. Venture capital firms and institutional investors, who are constantly seeking the next big opportunity, will naturally shift their focus to jurisdictions with more permissive or clearer regulatory frameworks. These investors are motivated by the potential for high returns, which is difficult to achieve in an environment that heavily restricts innovation and imposes substantial compliance costs. By making it difficult and expensive to operate within its borders, the U.S. makes itself a less attractive destination for the very capital needed to fuel the digital finance revolution.

Ultimately, this exodus of talent and capital will lead to an erosion of U.S. competitiveness in digital finance. While the U.S. has been a leader in financial technology for decades, other major economic blocs are now positioning themselves to lead in the digital asset space. The European Union, with its MiCA framework, and Asian hubs like Singapore and Hong Kong are developing their own stablecoin regulations that may be more balanced and globally interoperable. If the U.S. insists on an overly restrictive approach, it risks falling behind and losing its influence in setting global standards, thereby ceding its role in shaping the future of money and finance to other nations.

Countermeasures and Remaining Challenges

The drafters of the GENIUS Act were not oblivious to the risk of regulatory arbitrage and included provisions to address it. The Act attempts to exert extraterritorial reach by requiring foreign stablecoin issuers to register with the OCC and meet "comparable" regulatory standards if they wish to operate in the U.S. This is a clear attempt to close the door on jurisdiction shopping. However, enforcing such provisions across sovereign borders is an inherently challenging and often politically fraught process. Without robust international agreements, these measures are likely to be of limited effectiveness, leaving ample room for non-compliant actors to operate outside U.S. control.

To truly combat regulatory arbitrage, a robust system of international cooperation and harmonization of stablecoin regulations is required. The U.S. cannot regulate a global market in a vacuum. It would need to work closely with other major jurisdictions to create a unified framework. While this is the ideal solution, achieving global consensus on such detailed and complex financial frameworks is a lengthy and difficult process. This delay creates an interim period of uncertainty and fragmentation, which provides a perfect window of opportunity for regulatory arbitrage to flourish.

The core challenge for the GENIUS Act, and indeed for any stablecoin regulation, is finding the right balance between security and innovation. The Act's focus is clearly on achieving extreme stability and consumer protection through stringent, bank-like regulations. However, this approach risks stifling the very innovation that makes the digital asset space so dynamic and valuable. If the regulatory pendulum swings too far toward security, it will inevitably push some activity offshore, creating a less regulated global landscape for U.S. citizens to engage with. The most innovative and risk-tolerant projects will simply go where the rules are more accommodating.

This fundamental tension is nowhere more apparent than in the challenge posed by decentralized finance (DeFi). The GENIUS Act primarily targets centralized stablecoin issuers and Digital Asset Service Providers (DASPs), which have a physical or corporate presence. However, the inherently borderless and permissionless nature of DeFi means that it can operate outside of this centralized framework. U.S. persons can, and likely will, use DeFi protocols to access and use stablecoins that do not comply with the GENIUS Act, thereby operating outside the direct purview of U.S. regulation. This presents a persistent and ongoing challenge to the Act's comprehensive intent and underscores the difficulty of regulating a truly global and decentralized technology with a national legal framework.

Conclusion

The GENIUS Act's prescriptive and burdensome framework, while created with consumer protection in mind, unfortunately risks an offshore exodus that undermines its own goals. By imposing high compliance costs and rigid restrictions, the Act inadvertently favors a handful of established stablecoin issuers like Tether and Circle that possess the resources to navigate the regulatory maze. This approach risks stifling competition and innovation, ultimately benefiting a concentrated oligopoly rather than fostering a healthy and competitive market. The smaller, more agile firms and nascent startups that could drive the next wave of innovation are precisely the ones most likely to be forced offshore by the Act's punitive requirements.

This dynamic of regulatory favoritism will push a significant portion of the stablecoin market—and the talent and capital that support it—out of U.S.

jurisdiction. Stablecoin issuers, now classified as ABTs, will find it economically and operationally necessary to "jurisdiction shop," seeking more hospitable regulatory environments. The consequence will be a growing "shadow market" where U.S. users access non-compliant stablecoins through offshore exchanges and clever financial engineering, such as "wrapped" tokens. The U.S. will lose both the tax revenue and the supervisory oversight of this activity, creating a less transparent and more risky environment for its own citizens.

The GENIUS Act's attempt to exert extraterritorial reach through "comparable" regulatory standards is an imperfect and challenging solution. While well-intentioned, the enforcement of U.S. law across global borders is an immense and often futile undertaking, particularly in the borderless world of decentralized finance (DeFi). The fundamental disconnect lies in the Act's approach, which is heavily centralized and top-down, struggling to account for the inherently decentralized and permissionless nature of the technology it seeks to regulate.

A more effective model for stablecoin regulation can be found in the principles espoused by the DCBAS/UN model law on Digital Assets and Exchanged. Unlike the GENIUS Act, which is U.S.-centric and overly prescriptive, the DCBAS/UN framework focuses on creating a globally harmonized and technology-neutral approach. It prioritizes cross-border cooperation and interoperability, recognizing that digital assets are, by their nature, global. This model avoids regulatory overreach and the explicit favoritism seen in the GENIUS Act by promoting a level playing field for all participants, regardless of size or geographic location.

Ultimately, the DCBAS/UN model offers a constructive path forward by balancing the need for security with the imperative of innovation. By focusing on core principles of transparency, legal certainty, and international cooperation, it provides a flexible framework that can be adopted by diverse jurisdictions. This approach encourages, rather than stifles, the development of new and innovative stablecoin designs and applications. If the U.S. hopes to maintain its leadership role in digital finance, it must move beyond the restrictive framework of the GENIUS Act and embrace a more collaborative and forward-looking model that fosters innovation while effectively managing risk on a global scale.

Chapter 9: The Death of America's Vision as a Cryptocurrency Capital of the World.

"What we have done for ourselves dies with us; what we have done for others remains in this world and is immortal."

Albert Pike[12]

The passage of the GENIUS Act marks a watershed moment in the American approach to digital assets, providing a long-awaited regulatory framework for the burgeoning stablecoin market. However, a closer examination reveals a troubling reality: the Act's singular focus on "payment stablecoins" may be a classic case of misplaced priorities. While proponents argue that this focus brings much-needed clarity and stability to a key financial segment, critics contend it risks a strategic retreat from the broader, more innovative world of cryptocurrency, effectively narrowing the regulatory lens to a single, traditional use case. This myopic approach not only overlooks the vast potential of the wider crypto ecosystem but also signals a fundamental misunderstanding of the forces driving its most significant advancements.

The Act's narrow scope is evident in its prescriptive definition of what constitutes a "Permitted Payment Stablecoin." By concentrating on fiat-backed, 1:1,

---

[12] Staff (2025). "Death Quotes." Brainy Quote at https://www.brainyquote.com/topics/death-quotes.

traditionally-reserved tokens, the legislation creates a regulatory framework that is, at its core, an extension of the existing banking system. This approach may provide a sense of security, but it simultaneously ignores the diverse and vibrant applications of blockchain technology that exist far beyond simple payments. The crypto space is a hotbed of innovation encompassing everything from decentralized finance (DeFi) protocols to non-fungible tokens (NFTs), each with its own unique economic models and regulatory challenges. By dedicating its full attention to one small piece of this puzzle, the U.S. risks falling behind in the race to understand and govern the whole.

Furthermore, the Act's exclusionary provisions actively suppress certain forms of innovation. The explicit prohibition of algorithmic stablecoins, for instance, is a policy decision that closes the door on an entire class of financial engineering and theoretical development. Regardless of the market's past failures, this blanket ban stifles the potential for a new generation of more resilient and advanced designs. Similarly, the Act's restrictions on "yield" and other interactive functions severely limit how stablecoins can be used within DeFi ecosystems. By doing so, it ties the hands of developers and entrepreneurs who are building the financial systems of the future, compelling them to adhere to a restrictive, bank-centric model that is ill-suited to the permissionless and composable nature of Web3.

The concentration of regulatory energy on this narrow segment also has a less obvious, but equally damaging, consequence: the misallocation of limited government resources. Crafting and enforcing a highly prescriptive framework for stablecoins requires significant time, expertise, and capital from various regulatory bodies. This intense focus on one area may come at the expense of developing much-needed clarity and oversight for other critical sectors of the crypto economy. Without a comprehensive strategy for non-stablecoin cryptocurrencies, DeFi, tokenized securities, and decentralized autonomous organizations (DAOs), these areas remain in a state of regulatory limbo. This fragmentation hinders holistic growth and creates an environment of perpetual uncertainty, discouraging both innovators and investors.

The result is a regulatory paradigm that inadvertently stifles innovation by erecting high barriers to entry and limiting creative freedom. The bank-like requirements for becoming a Permitted Payment Stablecoin Issuer (PPSI) are so stringent and expensive that they effectively shut out startups and smaller fintechs. This creates a de facto consolidation of the market, where only a few large, well-capitalized institutions can afford to compete. The permissioned nature of this framework is a stark departure from the open, permissionless ethos that has fueled much of the crypto world's growth, and it undermines the very principles of decentralization that inspired the technology in the first place.

This misguided approach has a ripple effect that extends far beyond domestic policy. It is a catalyst for an offshore exodus of talent and capital, as entrepreneurs and investors seek more hospitable jurisdictions. The U.S. risks ceding its global leadership in digital finance to countries that are embracing a more holistic and forward-thinking regulatory model, such as the European Union's MiCA framework. By prioritizing a conservative and narrowly defined vision for stablecoins, the U.S. may be securing one small, traditional corner of the digital asset market while surrendering the future of the entire industry to its global competitors.

The Narrowing of "Crypto" to "Stablecoin Payments"

The GENIUS Act's primary regulatory thrust is a narrow, almost singular focus on payment stablecoins, defined as fiat-backed tokens with a 1:1 reserve ratio in highly liquid assets. While providing a clear path for this specific class of digital asset is a laudable goal, this overemphasis creates the risk of regulatory tunnel vision. The Act's framework, with its bank-like capital requirements and exhaustive disclosure mandates, fails to acknowledge the vast and varied ecosystem of other cryptocurrencies, such as utility tokens, governance tokens, and non-fungible tokens (NFTs), which have distinct functions and market dynamics. By creating a regulatory structure exclusively for a traditional payment function, the Act inadvertently suggests a lack of regulatory understanding or strategic interest in the broader innovation landscape that defines modern digital finance.

The exclusionary provisions within the Act further constrain the potential for innovation. The explicit ban on algorithmic stablecoins, for instance, irrespective of their design or potential for market resilience, effectively halts a significant area of research and development within the stablecoin sector. This is not just a matter of prudence but a rejection of a specific category of financial innovation. Furthermore, the prohibition on paying yield on stablecoin holdings and the tight restrictions on their use limit their integration with decentralized finance (DeFi) protocols, a key driver of growth and user adoption globally. This regulatory constraint pushes the U.S. market towards a conservative, bank-centric model, prioritizing traditional financial structures over the disruptive and potentially more efficient models that blockchain technology can offer.

By dedicating significant resources and regulatory attention to a highly prescriptive stablecoin framework, the Act may inadvertently starve other critical areas of the crypto economy of the regulatory clarity they desperately need. The long and complex process of building and implementing stablecoin regulations may divert attention from developing a comprehensive approach to spot markets for non-stablecoin cryptocurrencies, DeFi protocols, tokenized securities, and decentralized autonomous organizations (DAOs). This leaves these crucial sectors in a state of fragmented and uncertain supervision, hindering their ability to mature and scale within the U.S. and creating a piecemeal regulatory environment that is ill-equipped to handle the interconnected nature of the digital asset ecosystem.

Stifling Innovation Through High Barriers and Limited Freedom

The rigorous and expensive requirements for becoming a Permitted Payment Stablecoin Issuer (PPSI) create insurmountable barriers to entry for all but the most well-capitalized players. The mandated bank-like capital reserves, extensive reporting, and continuous auditing are so financially prohibitive that they effectively exclude startups, smaller fintechs, and crypto-native innovators. This framework, while designed to protect consumers, risks consolidating the stablecoin market in the hands of a few large, traditional financial institutions or major tech companies that have the resources to meet such demands. In doing so, it stifles competition and prevents the kind of dynamic innovation that often originates from smaller, more agile firms.

The permissioned nature of stablecoin issuance under the GENIUS Act stands in stark contrast to the permissionless ethos that has driven much of crypto innovation. The long regulatory approval cycles and continuous supervisory burden significantly slow down the pace of product development and experimentation. In an industry where rapid iteration and agile deployment are key to success, this regulatory inertia puts U.S. companies at a distinct disadvantage. It hinders the "build fast, break things" mentality that has historically defined the most innovative corners of the crypto world, locking the U.S. into a slower, more cautious development cycle while other global jurisdictions with lighter regulatory touch move ahead.

The Act's narrow scope also means it offers no clear regulatory pathway for the vast majority of the crypto market that falls outside the category of payment stablecoins. While it brings clarity for a specific type of digital asset, it leaves other foundational cryptocurrencies like Bitcoin and Ethereum, as well as a myriad of DeFi tokens and utility tokens, in a state of continued uncertainty. This absence of a holistic market structure acts as a powerful disincentive for building and investing in the U.S. The lack of a clear regulatory roadmap for these assets means entrepreneurs and investors will seek out jurisdictions that offer a more comprehensive and predictable environment, further contributing to a flight of innovation.

Driving Talent and Capital Offshore

A significant consequence of the GENIUS Act's restrictive approach is the inevitable brain drain and talent exodus. Highly skilled crypto developers, entrepreneurs, and researchers are drawn to environments where their work can thrive without excessive regulatory friction. If the U.S. is perceived as stifling to innovation and hostile to decentralized models, these talented individuals will increasingly choose to locate their operations in jurisdictions with more flexible, innovation-friendly, or established comprehensive crypto regulatory frameworks. This loss of human capital directly undermines the U.S.'s ability to remain at the forefront of blockchain and digital asset development, as the intellectual firepower that drives the industry finds more welcoming homes abroad.

This flight of talent is often mirrored by a corresponding capital flight and reduced domestic investment. Venture capital firms and institutional investors, who are always looking for the most promising and least friction-laden opportunities, will increasingly direct their investments toward crypto projects and companies operating outside the U.S. The high compliance costs, limited business models, and regulatory uncertainty created by the GENIUS Act make the U.S. a less attractive place for capital. This shift in investment allocation will starve domestic innovation and reduce the likelihood of groundbreaking crypto companies being founded and scaling within U.S. borders, ceding financial leadership to other global centers.

The regulatory contrast between the stringent U.S. regime and more permissive environments will inevitably lead to the emergence of offshore "crypto havens." These jurisdictions will attract businesses and users seeking less restrictive conditions, leading to a fragmentation of the global crypto market. The U.S. will likely control a highly regulated but potentially smaller piece of this market, while a significant portion of the most dynamic and innovative activity occurs beyond its direct purview. This regulatory arbitrage means that the U.S. will lose not only control but also the potential economic benefits and tax revenue from a thriving, global digital asset industry.

Eroding Global Leadership and Influence

By adopting a highly specific and restrictive stablecoin framework, the U.S. risks developing a model that is not easily interoperable or aligned with global best practices. As other major jurisdictions, such as the European Union with its Markets in Crypto-Assets (MiCA) regulation, develop more holistic and adaptable frameworks, the U.S. risks diminishing its influence in shaping future international standards. Instead of leading a coordinated, global effort, the U.S. may find itself with a domestic-centric model that isolates its own market, ceding leadership in defining the future of digital finance to regions with more comprehensive and forward-looking approaches.

The GENIUS Act largely favors traditional financial institutions as the preferred issuers of stablecoins, effectively integrating digital assets into existing banking structures rather than truly fostering new, decentralized models. While this ensures a measure of stability by reinforcing the current financial hierarchy, it undermines the very disruptive potential of blockchain technology. The Act's framework is fundamentally about bringing a new technology under old rules, rather than evolving the rules to meet the technology. This approach may ensure the U.S. remains a global banking capital, but it actively works against the vision of becoming a true cryptocurrency capital, which would require embracing more decentralized and innovative paradigms.

Despite its stated goal of bringing regulatory clarity, the Act's restrictive nature for stablecoins, combined with the continued lack of a comprehensive regulatory plan for the broader crypto market, might be perceived by the global crypto community as a hostile or unwelcoming stance from the U.S. This perception, whether intended or not, can deter future investment, partnership, and talent flow into the country. The U.S. has long been a destination for technological innovation, but by signaling a narrow, conservative, and permissioned approach to digital assets, it risks eroding that reputation and losing its long-term vision for leadership in the digital finance space.

Conclusion

The GENIUS Act's narrow focus on payment stablecoins, while offering a clear pathway for a specific segment of the market, reveals a fundamental flaw in the U.S. regulatory strategy for digital assets. By over-emphasizing a traditional, bank-centric model, the Act has created a framework that is more about containment than about cultivation. It prioritizes stability at the expense of innovation, a trade-off that will have profound long-term consequences for the U.S.'s competitive standing in the global digital economy. The Act's restrictive nature, coupled with its failure to address the wider crypto ecosystem, represents a missed opportunity to establish a truly holistic and forward-thinking regulatory model.

The direct result of this narrow approach is the creation of a high-friction environment that stifles innovation at its source. The exorbitant compliance costs and stringent requirements for becoming a Permitted Payment Stablecoin Issuer (PPSI) effectively erect a barrier to entry that consolidates the market in the hands of a few large, well-resourced players. This lack of competition and the permissioned nature of the framework are antithetical to the principles of decentralization and open innovation that have been the lifeblood of the crypto industry. The U.S. is trading the dynamic, permissionless innovation of the global crypto market for a secure but static domestic market dominated by a handful of established financial giants.

Furthermore, the Act's singular focus on payment stablecoins creates a regulatory vacuum for the vast majority of the crypto market. By dedicating so much energy to one limited area, regulators have left the rest of the ecosystem—including DeFi, NFTs, and other digital assets—in a state of continued uncertainty and fragmentation. This incomplete regulatory picture is a significant disincentive for investors and developers, who thrive on predictability and clear rules of the road. This uncertainty is a powerful catalyst for driving innovation and capital offshore to jurisdictions that have embraced a more comprehensive regulatory philosophy.

The most damaging consequence of this misguided policy is the erosion of U.S. global leadership. The flight of talent and capital to more hospitable jurisdictions is not a theoretical risk but an ongoing reality. As skilled developers and venture capital move to places like the EU, which has a more comprehensive framework with its MiCA regulation, the U.S. risks ceding its influence in setting international standards for digital finance. The world is watching to see how major economic powers will approach this new technology, and by focusing so narrowly on one use case, the U.S. is signaling a retreat from the broader, more revolutionary aspects of the industry.

The Act's inherent bias towards traditional financial institutions also undermines the disruptive potential of blockchain technology. By reinforcing the existing financial hierarchy and simply adding a digital layer to it, the U.S. is missing the opportunity to foster new, decentralized models that could fundamentally reshape finance. The true power of crypto lies in its ability to disintermediate and create more efficient, permissionless systems. The GENIUS Act, in its current form, largely ignores this potential, instead focusing on making the old system work a little more smoothly, rather than building the foundations for a new one.

In the end, the GENIUS Act may provide stability for one small corner of the crypto world, but it does so at the cost of the entire ecosystem's long-term health and growth within the U.S. The Act's narrow scope, exclusionary policies, and high barriers to entry collectively serve to stifle innovation, drive talent and capital abroad, and diminish America's global influence in a critical technological frontier. A more balanced and forward-looking approach is needed—one that recognizes the diversity and potential of the entire crypto space, rather than just a single, traditional application. Only then can the U.S. hope to truly lead the digital finance revolution and build a regulatory framework that is both secure and conducive to innovation.

Part II: Advanced Stablecoin Methodologies Hampered by GENIUS Act

Chapter 10: Stablecoin 1.0, 1.1 and 1.5, Keeping the 386 of digital assets alive

“The way to crush the bourgeoisie is to grind them between the millstones of taxation and inflation.”

Vladimir Lenin[13]

The GENIUS Act’s approach to stablecoin regulation is a case study in how new technology can be retrofitted into an outdated, conservative framework. While the Act is lauded for bringing long-awaited clarity to the digital asset space, its methodology is fundamentally about preserving the past, not building for the future. By heavily promoting stablecoin models 1.0 and 1.1—tokens backed by fiat currency and short-term Treasury bonds, respectively—the legislation effectively "keeps the 386 alive," a metaphor for clinging to legacy systems in the face of a new era of digital evolution. This focus on a narrow, proven path stifles the very innovation that is needed to secure the U.S.’s long-term leadership in the global digital economy.

The "386" analogy is a poignant one, referencing an era of computing that, while revolutionary for its time, is now a distant memory. Similarly, the GENIUS Act’s framework for stablecoins is built around concepts that are a digital mirror of traditional, conservative financial products. Stablecoin 1.0, the fiat-backed

[13] Staff (2025). “Inflation Quotes.” Brainy Quote at https://www.brainyquote.com/topics/inflation-quotes.

token, is simply a digital version of cash held in a vault. Stablecoin 1.1, backed by short-term Treasuries, is a tokenized money market fund. The Act's genius, therefore, is not in fostering a new type of digital money but in finding a way to make old financial concepts compliant and operational on a blockchain.

This conservative methodology is most apparent in the Act's prescriptive rules regarding reserve assets. By mandating that "payment stablecoins" must be backed 1:1 by highly specific High-Quality Liquid Assets (HQLAs), the Act entrenches the fiat-backed (1.0) and Treasury-backed (1.1) models as the only acceptable forms of digital stability. While this approach prioritizes safety and aligns with traditional banking principles, it simultaneously signals a disinterest in, or a fundamental fear of, alternative reserve mechanisms that could be more efficient or innovative. The result is a regulatory environment that rewards a lack of creativity, ensuring that the U.S. stablecoin market will be dominated by a few conservative, traditional designs.

Furthermore, the Act's stance on more complex, yet potentially more robust, stablecoin models is illuminating. Stablecoin 1.5, often referred to as a basket stablecoin, is a token whose value is pegged to a basket of fiat currencies. While the GENIUS Act doesn't explicitly prohibit these tokens, its rigid rules make them incredibly difficult to implement. The requirement to maintain 1:1 HQLA reserves for each component of the basket adds immense operational complexity and regulatory overhead, pushing these potentially more resilient and diversified models to the periphery. The Act essentially permits an "old" idea from traditional currency management to exist digitally, but without offering any of the benefits of a truly native digital design.

Beyond these specific provisions, the Act's overall structure favors incumbent financial institutions. The extensive regulatory and compliance burdens of becoming a Permitted Payment Stablecoin Issuer (PPSI) are so high that they are only feasible for large, well-capitalized banks and fintechs. This approach funnels stablecoin innovation through the existing, often slow and costly, financial infrastructure, hindering the broader, more disruptive potential of blockchain technology. Instead of fostering a genuinely new, digitally native financial system, the Act simply retrofits a new coat of paint onto the legacy "386-era" financial plumbing.

Ultimately, by doubling down on these outdated models, the GENIUS Act risks a major strategic misstep. The U.S. is securing a safe but conservative corner of the stablecoin market while other jurisdictions, with more flexible and forward-thinking frameworks, are positioned to become the hubs for next-generation digital asset innovation. The Act is not a framework for global leadership but a roadmap for becoming a follower. The focus on what is proven safe, rather than what is creatively possible, could ultimately limit the U.S.'s long-term competitive edge and cede critical ground in the evolving global digital economy.

The Mandate for Fiat and Treasury Backing: The Digital Dollar 1.0

The GENIUS Act's methodology for promoting outdated stablecoins is clearly articulated in its definition of permissible reserve assets. The Act's insistence that "payment stablecoins" must be backed 1:1 by "High-Quality Liquid Assets" (HQLAs) serves to codify the most conservative stablecoin models. The specific inclusion of U.S. currency and short-term U.S. Treasury securities (93 days or less) as the primary HQLAs directly props up fiat-backed (1.0) and Treasury-backed (1.1) stablecoins. This approach essentially takes the existing, traditional financial models of holding cash or investing in a money market fund and requires that stablecoins must adhere to them. While this ensures a level of safety and stability, it also entrenches these established methods as the only acceptable form of digital stability, thereby stifling innovation in alternative backing mechanisms and preventing the evolution of more sophisticated designs.

The prohibition on stablecoin issuers from offering yield is a further example of the Act's conservative bias. By a core tenet, Permitted Payment Stablecoin Issuers (PPSIs) are forbidden from offering interest or yield to holders solely for holding the coin. This rule reinforces the "digital cash" or "tokenized deposit" model, making stablecoins analogous to holding non-interest-bearing physical cash or a zero-interest checking account. This regulatory stance prevents stablecoins from becoming more dynamic, yield-generating instruments that leverage blockchain capabilities for productive use. As a result, stablecoins are limited to a simple, non-productive store of value for transactional purposes, which limits their competitiveness against yield-bearing alternatives in both traditional and decentralized finance and solidifies a conservative vision for their role in the economy.

Basket Stablecoins: A Niche Allowed, But Under Strict Controls

While the GENIUS Act's primary focus is on stablecoins pegged to a single fiat currency, its definition of "fixed monetary value" implicitly allows for stablecoins pegged to a basket of fiat currencies (often considered Stablecoin 1.5). As long as the issuer can demonstrate an obligation to redeem the token for a fixed value relative to that basket and maintains 1:1 HQLA reserves for each component, it could theoretically qualify. However, this is not an endorsement of a new idea but a permission for an old one. Basket stablecoins have existed as a concept in currency management for decades. The Act allows for this older idea to be digitally wrapped, but it does so without offering any new, digitally native advantages, and the immense operational and regulatory complexity of managing such a system under the Act's rules makes it highly unlikely to become a dominant force.

The challenges in HQLA management for these basket stablecoins make them a niche offering at best. Managing a 1:1 reserve for a basket of fiat currencies—each potentially requiring its own HQLA set within their respective jurisdictions and adhering to U.S.-centric rules—adds immense complexity. The Act's focus on U.S. HQLAs would make a multi-currency basket exceptionally difficult to implement for a U.S. PPSI. This complexity effectively pushes these stablecoins further into the realm of traditional, multi-currency banking operations and away from agile digital innovation. It reinforces a reliance on established (and often slow) financial mechanisms rather than fostering a new paradigm for digital stability and efficiency.

Consolidation and Resistance to Digital Evolution

The extensive regulatory and compliance burdens of the GENIUS Act create a disproportionate advantage for large, existing financial institutions. These entities already have the established compliance departments, legal teams, and capital reserves necessary to become Permitted Payment Stablecoin Issuers (PPSIs). This regulatory framework, therefore, favors the incumbents, effectively turning stablecoin issuance into an extension of traditional banking services. This approach funnels stablecoin innovation through the existing financial infrastructure, which is often criticized for its slowness and high costs. The Act is not fostering a genuinely new, digitally native financial system but is instead retrofitting stablecoins into the legacy financial plumbing, hindering the broader, more disruptive potential of blockchain technology.

By rigidly defining "payment stablecoin" and permissible reserves, the Act actively suppresses experimentation and true crypto-native designs. The legislation discourages or outright prohibits innovative approaches to stability, such as algorithmic models or those that leverage crypto-native collateral. This strategy eliminates any competitive pressure from potentially more efficient or fundamentally different stablecoin designs. It ensures that the U.S. market will be predominantly composed of stablecoins that are essentially tokenized versions of very traditional, low-risk financial instruments. This solidifies a conservative, "safe," but potentially less ambitious vision for stablecoins in the U.S., limiting the industry's ability to explore the full spectrum of innovation that the cryptocurrency space offers.

The Act’s restrictive nature, while ensuring stability for fiat-backed stablecoins, means the U.S. may miss the opportunity to lead in the development and regulation of truly next-generation, digitally native stablecoins. Other jurisdictions with more flexible frameworks might become the hubs for such innovation, attracting the talent and capital needed to push the boundaries of the technology. By doubling down on the "386-era" model, the U.S. risks becoming a follower rather than a leader in future stablecoin advancements, potentially ceding critical ground in the evolving global digital economy. The focus on what is proven safe, rather than what is innovatively possible, could ultimately limit the U.S.'s long-term competitive edge in this critical technological frontier.

Conclusion

The GENIUS Act's methodology reveals a profound tension between the need for regulatory clarity and the desire for innovation. Instead of creating a framework that would allow the digital asset space to evolve, the Act has chosen a path that explicitly favors and reinforces outdated stablecoin models 1.0 and 1.1. By mandating rigid, bank-like reserve requirements and prohibiting yield, it has defined the ideal "payment stablecoin" as a tokenized version of a traditional, non-productive financial instrument. This approach, while providing a sense of security, fundamentally misunderstands the ethos of digital innovation and the potential for new, more dynamic forms of money.

The Act's conservative bias is not only evident in what it mandates but also in what it implicitly discourages. While not explicitly banning more sophisticated designs like basket stablecoins (Stablecoin 1.5), the legislation's prescriptive rules on HQLA management create operational hurdles so immense that they effectively sideline these models. The result is a regulatory environment where an "old" idea can exist digitally, but without the benefit of a truly native design, reinforcing a reliance on established and often slow multi-currency financial mechanisms rather than agile digital innovation.

Furthermore, the extensive regulatory burden and compliance costs of the GENIUS Act disproportionately favor large, incumbent financial institutions. This approach stifles competition, consolidates the stablecoin market, and ensures that innovation is funneled through the existing financial infrastructure. By retrofitting stablecoins into the "386-era" financial plumbing, the Act hinders the development of a genuinely new, digitally native financial system and suppresses the experimentation that could lead to more efficient and fundamentally different stablecoin designs. The U.S. is choosing to preserve the old system rather than enable a new one.

The long-term consequences of this strategy are significant. By doubling down on a conservative model, the U.S. is not setting the stage for future leadership but is risking a brain drain of talent and a flight of capital to more flexible jurisdictions. As other countries develop more comprehensive and forward-thinking frameworks that embrace the full spectrum of digital asset innovation, the U.S. may find itself with a safe but stagnant market. Its focus on what is proven safe, rather than what is innovatively possible, could ultimately limit its competitive edge in the global digital economy.

In conclusion, the GENIUS Act, in its current form, is a regulatory monument to the past. It's a bill designed to "keep the 386 alive," ensuring the dominance of traditional financial concepts in the digital age. By rigidly defining stablecoins and limiting their potential, the Act has missed a critical opportunity to lead in the development of next-generation digital finance. While it provides a semblance of clarity and stability for a specific segment of the market, it does so at the cost of genuine innovation, and this strategic misstep may prove to be the most significant consequence of the legislation.

Chapter 11: Undermining Algorithmic Tokens

"You want to evaluate future [users], but in order to train an algorithm that will help you identify future defaults, you have to train it and evaluate it on past data."

Anthony Goldbloom[14]

The GENIUS Act, while presented as a comprehensive framework for the regulation of digital assets, can be viewed through a more critical lens as a deliberate and targeted attack on algorithmic stablecoins. This is not simply a matter of a new law failing to account for a novel technology; rather, the Act's provisions are meticulously crafted to render these tokens non-compliant. The core reason for this direct assault is that algorithmic stablecoins pose a fundamental threat not to the stability of a single currency, but to the entire debt-backed credit system that underpins traditional banking. By operating independently of bank deposits or government-issued debt, these tokens represent a parallel monetary primitive that could, if successful, diminish the power and necessity of legacy financial institutions.

At its heart, the traditional banking system functions by creating credit and money from debt. Commercial banks loan out money, creating new deposits that are

---

[14] Staff (2025). "Algorithm Quotes." Brainy Quote at https://www.brainyquote.com/topics/algorithm-quotes.

a form of money, all based on a fractional reserve system. Similarly, central bank actions, such as quantitative easing, often involve the purchase of government debt to inject liquidity into the system. Algorithmic stablecoins, on the other hand, operate on a different paradigm. Their stability is maintained through a combination of on-chain collateral and automated smart contract logic, not through a central issuer holding off-chain, government-backed assets. This entirely different mechanism for monetary creation and stability is what makes them such a profound threat, as they represent a form of capital that operates outside of the debt-based system.

The GENIUS Act's methodology, therefore, is a strategic response to this threat. By narrowly defining "payment stablecoins" and mandating that they must be backed 1:1 by "High-Quality Liquid Assets" (HQLAs) like U.S. currency and short-term Treasuries, the Act creates a definitional moat that no algorithmic token can cross. This isn't an oversight; it's a deliberate choice to ensure that any stablecoin operating in the U.S. remains tethered to the traditional financial system. In essence, the Act is not just regulating an asset but dictating its very architecture, forcing it to be a digital extension of a bank deposit or a money market fund, and thereby preserving the existing order.

This regulatory maneuver also extends to the very structure of the issuers themselves. The Act's requirement for a central, accountable "Permitted

Payment Stablecoin Issuer" (PPSI) with the capabilities to "seize, freeze, or burn" tokens is directly antithetical to the decentralized, censorship-resistant design of many algorithmic stablecoins. These provisions are not merely about consumer protection or sanctions compliance; they are about control. By mandating a centralized point of failure and control, the Act ensures that any compliant stablecoin can be influenced and governed by the legacy financial system, effectively undermining the core tenets of decentralization that make algorithmic tokens so revolutionary.

Chapter 11 will delve into the specific mechanisms through which the GENIUS Act executes this strategic dismantling of algorithmic tokens. From the explicit exclusion in its definitions to the incompatibility with its reserve requirements and the contradiction of its issuer mandates, we will explore how the Act systematically closes every possible pathway for these innovative designs to operate within the U.S. regulatory framework. The chapter will demonstrate that the GENIUS Act is not a neutral piece of legislation but a clear and direct attack on a technology that threatens to build a parallel, non-debt-based financial system.

Definitional Incompatibility and the Mandate for Traditional Reserves

The GENIUS Act's definition of a "payment stablecoin" is the first step in its systematic undermining of algorithmic tokens. The Act defines such a coin as a digital asset where an issuer is obligated to convert it for a fixed amount of monetary value, and it must be backed 1:1 by "High-Quality Liquid Assets" (HQLAs). This is a direct attack because algorithmic stablecoins are fundamentally different. They do not rely on a central issuer holding a direct 1:1 backing with off-chain assets. Instead, they maintain their peg through automated, on-chain mechanisms that manage supply and demand, often using a volatile "companion" asset. This fundamental difference means they cannot meet the Act's core definitional and reserve requirements.

The HQLA requirement in the GENIUS Act directly conflicts with the collateral structures of virtually all algorithmic stablecoins. The Act's strict list of permissible reserve assets—such as cash and short-term Treasuries—is a stark contrast to the volatile cryptocurrencies (like Bitcoin, Ethereum, or a native governance token) or complex debt mechanisms that serve as backing for algorithmic tokens. This is a deliberate undermining of the technology; even if an algorithmic stablecoin were "over-collateralized" with crypto assets, those assets are not considered HQLAs under the Act. This renders any algorithmic stablecoin design inherently non-compliant for operation as a "payment stablecoin" in the U.S., effectively making them illegal for use in the mainstream financial system. This is a direct shot at technologies like TerraUSD (UST), which used an algorithmic relationship with its governance token, LUNA, to maintain its peg, and Dai (DAI), which, while over-collateralized, uses crypto assets that fall outside the Act's HQLA definition.

Lack of Centralized Issuer Accountability and Control

The GENIUS Act requires that only regulated entities—either bank subsidiaries or qualified non-banks—can be "Permitted Payment Stablecoin Issuers" (PPSIs). This requirement for a central, identifiable legal entity is a direct attack on the decentralized nature of many algorithmic stablecoins, which are designed to be governed by smart contracts and community proposals. This absence of a traditional "issuer" makes it impossible for these projects to apply for, or comply with, the PPSI framework. By mandating a centralized issuer, the Act forces a level of control and accountability that is antithetical to the core philosophy of decentralization and censorship resistance.

Furthermore, the Act's requirement for PPSIs to have the technical capability to "seize, freeze, or burn" stablecoins under lawful orders is a direct contradiction to the core principles of decentralization. A truly decentralized algorithmic stablecoin, by its very design, should not have a central party with such override capabilities. This provision is not a simple regulatory measure; it is a mandate for centralized control that undermines the fundamental design ethos of most algorithmic stablecoins. Any project designed for true decentralization would struggle or fail to meet this requirement, effectively making it a non-starter for the U.S. market.

Business Model Incompatibility and Secondary Market Sunset

The GENIUS Act's prohibition on yield and lending mechanisms is another way it undermines algorithmic stablecoins. The Act explicitly forbids PPSIs from paying interest or yield to stablecoin holders solely for holding the coin. This is a critical blow to many algorithmic stablecoin models, which rely on complex lending, borrowing, or staking mechanisms (often involving their companion tokens) that implicitly or explicitly offer yield as a central part of their peg-maintenance strategy. These yield-generating features, which are vital to the economic incentives of many algorithmic designs, would be non-compliant under the GENIUS Act's "no yield" rule, effectively destroying their business model.

Finally, the Act includes a three-year sunset clause that will eventually prohibit Digital Asset Service Providers (DASPs) from offering or selling non-compliant payment stablecoins to U.S. persons. This creates a hard deadline for any existing algorithmic stablecoin to either transform itself into a GENIUS-compliant PPSI—which is practically impossible given the other sections of the Act—or face being blacklisted from the mainstream U.S. market. This provision forces exchanges and other service providers to delist these tokens, making them illiquid and unusable for U.S. residents through regulated channels. This is a direct and forceful attack on their viability, affecting projects like Fei Protocol (FEI), USDD, and MIM, whose business models would be rendered non-compliant by the Act’s strict rules and regulations.

Conclusion

The GENIUS Act is not a neutral piece of legislation; it is a calculated and comprehensive effort to protect the traditional, debt-based financial system from a potent new form of digital money. The Act's narrow definition of a "payment stablecoin" and its mandate for 1:1 HQLA backing deliberately exclude algorithmic tokens, which are designed to operate independently of off-chain assets and government debt. This definitional incompatibility, coupled with the explicit prohibition on crypto-native collateral, is a clear sign that the Act's drafters were not simply focused on safety, but on ensuring that any compliant digital asset must serve as an extension of the legacy financial system.

This strategic attack extends beyond mere definitions to the very structure of the tokens and their issuers. By requiring a centralized "Permitted Payment Stablecoin Issuer" (PPSI) with the ability to "seize, freeze, or burn" tokens, the Act demands a level of control that is fundamentally incompatible with the decentralized, censorship-resistant design of algorithmic stablecoins. This is not about consumer protection; it is about ensuring that a central point of authority—and therefore a central point of control by the government and financial institutions—remains over the monetary supply, something that decentralized, algorithmic tokens are designed to resist.

The Act's attack is also a direct strike at the business models that underpin many algorithmic tokens. By prohibiting yield for holding a stablecoin, it invalidates the very economic incentives that many of these designs use to maintain their peg. The three-year sunset clause is the final nail in the coffin, creating an existential deadline for any non-compliant token. This is not a policy of cautious regulation but a policy of deliberate destruction, designed to cleanse the market of any token that could challenge the traditional banking model.

Ultimately, the GENIUS Act's methodology is a vivid example of a legacy system defending itself against a disruptive innovation. The central fear is not a stablecoin de-pegging, but a stablecoin succeeding on its own terms—without reliance on bank deposits, government treasuries, or centralized control. A truly successful algorithmic token would represent a new monetary primitive, a form of capital created outside the debt-credit cycle, which would fundamentally alter the balance of power in the financial world.

The long-term consequence of this defensive posture is a significant opportunity cost for the U.S. While the Act ensures a "safe" and compliant stablecoin market, it cedes leadership in the development of a more innovative and potentially more resilient financial infrastructure to other jurisdictions. The U.S. is choosing to reinforce its existing financial plumbing rather than building a next-generation system from the ground up, and this strategic misstep may have profound implications for its future competitiveness in the global digital economy.

This chapter demonstrates that the GENIUS Act is not a benign regulatory framework. It is a strategic, defensive maneuver by an established financial order against a technology that poses a fundamental threat to its very existence. The systematic undermining of algorithmic stablecoins is not an accident of legislation but a deliberate choice to preserve the past at the expense of a potentially more innovative, and more decentralized, financial future.

Chapter 12: Stablecoin 1.3, 1.6 & 1.8 - Single and Multi-Stock Based Security Tokens and Derivative Based Tokens

“By a continuing process of inflation, government can confiscate, secretly and unobserved, an important part of the wealth of their citizens.”

John Maynard Keynes[15]

The GENIUS Act’s conservative framework for stablecoins is most glaring in its silent but definitive exclusion of a powerful category of digital assets: those pegged to real-world assets like stocks or complex financial instruments like derivatives. This chapter examines how stablecoins 1.3 (single-stock based), 1.6 (multi-stock/derivative-based), and 1.8 (purely derivative-based) are systematically undermined by the Act. By narrowly defining "payment stablecoins" and mandating off-chain, fiat-based reserves, the legislation effectively creates a regulatory moat that these innovative designs cannot cross. The result is not merely a lack of support, but an outright prohibition by definitional exclusion, stifling a vast area of financial engineering and innovation before it can even begin.

At the core of this issue is the Act's rigid focus on "fixed monetary value" and "High-Quality Liquid Assets" (HQLAs). A stablecoin pegged to the value of

---

[15] Staff (2025). “Inflation Quotes.” Brainy Quote at https://www.brainyquote.com/topics/inflation-quotes.

a basket of stocks, such as the S&P 500, offers a different kind of stability—a hedge against inflation and a reflection of real economic growth—but it is not pegged to a "fixed monetary value" like the U.S. dollar. Similarly, the underlying assets of these stablecoins, such as equities or derivatives, are not considered HQLAs under the Act's narrow definition, which is limited to U.S. currency and short-term Treasuries. This creates a fundamental incompatibility that is both intentional and strategic, forcing stablecoin innovation to remain within the confines of traditional, fiat-backed models.

The implications of this exclusion are far-reaching. By tethering all regulated stablecoins to a single fiat currency, the GENIUS Act inadvertently locks the entire digital asset ecosystem into the inherent vulnerabilities of that currency. This means that a compliant stablecoin, while "stable" in nominal dollar terms, is still susceptible to the long-term devaluation of the dollar due to inflation and the unpredictable effects of central bank monetary policies like Quantitative Easing (QE). The very stablecoins that could offer a hedge against these risks—those backed by real assets or derivative strategies—are the ones being prevented from gaining a foothold in the U.S. market.

Ultimately, the Act's methodology reveals a profound lack of foresight. While it prioritizes a conservative approach to ensure short-term stability and consumer protection, it misses a critical opportunity to position the U.S. as a leader in a more resilient and sophisticated digital financial future. By banning these advanced stablecoin designs, the Act cedes this entire domain of financial engineering to other jurisdictions, risking that the U.S. becomes a consumer rather than a creator of the next generation of financial technology. This is a strategic misstep that may prove costly in the long run.

The Exclusionary Definition of "Payment Stablecoin" and Reserves

The GENIUS Act's definition of "payment stablecoins" as those redeemable 1:1 for a "fixed monetary value" and backed by "High-Quality Liquid Assets" (HQLAs) fundamentally excludes innovative tokens like those based on stocks or derivatives. This is a deliberate act of regulatory damage. A stablecoin pegged to a basket of stocks (Stablecoin 1.6), or one that relies on complex derivative strategies (Stablecoin 1.8) for its stability, cannot meet these requirements. The assets that underpin these tokens—stocks, options, and other derivatives—are not on the Act's approved list of HQLAs, which is limited to U.S. currency and short-term Treasuries. This isn't just a lack of support for these models; it's an outright prohibition by exclusion, preventing any such design from operating as a "payment stablecoin" in the U.S.

The Act's explicit prohibition on paying interest or yield to stablecoin holders is particularly damaging to derivative-based models. Many sophisticated derivative-based stablecoins might aim to generate yield as part of their pegging mechanism, using it as a way to attract liquidity or incentivize certain behaviors. The Act's blanket "no yield" prohibition directly undermines these innovative structures, forcing any compliant stablecoin into a non-productive, digital cash-like form. Such a model inherently loses purchasing power during inflationary periods, as it cannot offer any mechanism for its holders to hedge against the devaluation of the underlying fiat currency, thus destroying its primary utility.

Locking into Fiat's Inherent Vulnerabilities

By mandating a direct 1:1 peg to a single fiat currency, the GENIUS Act locks stablecoins into the inherent vulnerabilities of that currency, namely inflation and devaluation. A "stable" dollar-pegged stablecoin is only as stable as the dollar itself. This means that while its nominal value remains constant, its real purchasing power erodes over time due to inflation. This provision prevents potentially more resilient designs—such as stablecoins backed by a diversified basket of stocks or commodities—from gaining traction in the U.S. market. These alternatives could theoretically offer a hedge against fiat inflation, aiming for "real" purchasing power stability rather than just nominal dollar stability, but the Act forces users into an inflationary digital asset.

Furthermore, the Act's compliant stablecoins are completely susceptible to central bank monetary policies, such as Quantitative Easing (QE). When the money supply is increased, the value of each unit of currency is diluted, a risk that a GENIUS Act-compliant stablecoin cannot protect its holders from. In contrast, a stock-based stablecoin could offer exposure to asset appreciation that might offset currency debasement, while derivative-based stablecoins could be constructed to directly hedge against specific monetary policy risks. The Act ensures that stablecoin users are entirely exposed to the whims of central bank policy, missing a key opportunity for digital assets to offer a form of value transfer that is more independent.

The Act's reinforcement of the link between stablecoins and traditional fiat also makes them vulnerable to general corruption and political influence. Fiat currencies and the systems that govern them are tied to political decisions and potential corruption within traditional financial institutions. Stablecoins backed by assets less directly controlled by government monetary policy, or those that leverage transparent on-chain derivative contracts, could offer a degree of independence from these risks. By reinforcing the link to fiat and traditional banking, the GENIUS Act misses an opportunity for stablecoins to offer a more robust or politically neutral form of digital value transfer, a key value proposition of the broader crypto space.

Stifling Innovation Beyond the "Digital Dollar"

The GENIUS Act's narrow scope actively suppresses the emergence of stablecoins designed for diverse hedging strategies. For example, a stablecoin pegged to an inflation-indexed bond or a basket of commodities could offer a more nuanced form of "stability" relevant to different economic conditions. However, the Act's rigid definition and reserve requirements render such ideas non-compliant. This limitation hinders the development of a richer stablecoin ecosystem where users could choose stablecoins that reflect their specific risk appetite and economic outlook, effectively limiting stablecoins to a one-size-fits-all "digital dollar" model that may not be optimal for everyone.

The crypto space has seen rapid innovation in tokenized derivatives and complex financial instruments. Stablecoins backed by these derivatives could offer new ways to manage risk or achieve stability through dynamic strategies. Unfortunately, the GENIUS Act's conservative approach and focus on simple 1:1 HQLA backing effectively bans most forms of derivative-backed stablecoins from operating in the U.S. This cuts off a significant area of financial engineering that could have otherwise found a legitimate home in the regulated U.S. market, thereby stifling a crucial avenue of innovation.

Furthermore, the Act's strict reserve requirements implicitly disincentivize the tokenization of a broader range of real-world assets, such as real estate, commodities, or equities, as potential stablecoin collateral or pegs. While not directly a stablecoin, the development of robust, liquid markets for tokenized real assets could pave the way for stablecoins whose value is derived from these more diverse and inflation-resistant sources. The GENIUS Act's narrow focus on fiat and Treasuries deters this broader tokenization trend within the regulated U.S. stablecoin landscape, limiting the potential of the entire ecosystem.

The Strategic Cost to America's Crypto Leadership

By heavily restricting alternative stablecoin designs, the GENIUS Act risks pushing sophisticated financial engineering and the development of non-fiat-pegged stablecoins to more permissive jurisdictions. This means that if stablecoins backed by stocks or derivatives prove valuable and resilient elsewhere, the U.S. will be a consumer, not a leader, in those innovations. This is a significant strategic risk that could cede a key area of future financial technology to other countries.

Despite the stated goal of making the U.S. a crypto capital, the Act's conservative nature might solidify a perception that the U.S. is cautious to the point of stifling genuine innovation beyond replicating traditional financial instruments in digital form. This could deter talent and capital from entering the U.S. crypto space, as the most ambitious and creative minds in the industry seek environments where their ideas can be legally and commercially viable. This reinforces a reputation as a digital laggard, which could be difficult to reverse.

In an era of increasing global economic volatility, central bank independence concerns, and persistent inflation, alternative stablecoin designs could offer valuable tools for individuals and institutions seeking to preserve purchasing power or diversify risk. By locking stablecoins to fiat, the U.S. limits the tools available to its citizens to navigate these macroeconomic challenges through digital assets. This is a critical missed opportunity that could have provided a form of financial resilience and independence for citizens.

Finally, the GENIUS Act is a political compromise, prioritizing the immediate concerns of financial stability and consumer protection over the long-term potential for disruptive and truly innovative stablecoin designs. This leads to a regulatory framework that might be "safe" but lacks foresight and adaptability. By choosing a politically expedient solution, the Act sacrifices the possibility of a more optimal design that could have harnessed the full potential of blockchain technology. The result is a system that might be stable in the short term but is fundamentally unprepared for the future.

Conclusion

The GENIUS Act's narrow and restrictive framework is a fundamental failure of regulatory imagination. Its systematic exclusion of stablecoins 1.3, 1.6, and 1.8—those based on stocks, derivatives, and a combination of both—is a direct consequence of its rigid adherence to outdated financial models. By defining "payment stablecoin" so narrowly and demanding reserve assets that are limited to fiat and short-term Treasuries, the Act creates an insurmountable barrier for any design that seeks to derive its stability from a broader, more innovative range of real-world or crypto-native assets. This is not a mistake; it is a deliberate regulatory choice to preserve the primacy of the fiat-backed financial system.

A key consequence of this approach is that the Act locks stablecoins, and by extension their users, into the inherent vulnerabilities of a single fiat currency. A GENIUS Act-compliant stablecoin is little more than a tokenized bank deposit, offering no protection against the long-term erosion of purchasing power from inflation or the unpredictable effects of central bank monetary policies like Quantitative Easing. By effectively banning stablecoins that could offer a hedge against these very risks—such as those backed by real assets or sophisticated derivative strategies—the Act denies individuals and institutions a critical tool for economic resilience in an era of increasing volatility.

This strategic failure to embrace diverse stablecoin designs also represents a significant missed opportunity for the U.S. to lead in a critical area of financial technology. By limiting stablecoins to a "one-size-fits-all" digital dollar model, the Act stifles a whole category of sophisticated financial engineering and real-world asset tokenization. Instead of being a hub for innovation in stablecoins that could offer stability through exposure to equities, commodities, or complex derivatives, the U.S. is signaling that its regulatory environment is hostile to such creativity, and this may push the most ambitious projects to other, more permissive jurisdictions.

The result is a reinforcement of a perception that the U.S. is a regulatory laggard, more concerned with cautious preservation than with bold, forward-looking innovation. Despite the stated goals of making the U.S. a crypto capital, the Act's conservative nature and its focus on a "safe" but limited stablecoin model may deter the very talent and capital it seeks to attract. The long-term economic and geopolitical costs of this approach could be substantial, as other nations may seize the opportunity to develop and regulate the next generation of financial technology that the U.S. has explicitly chosen to ignore.

In conclusion, the GENIUS Act's handling of stablecoins 1.3, 1.6, and 1.8 is a microcosm of its broader philosophical flaws. It is a piece of legislation born from political compromise that prioritizes immediate financial stability over long-term, innovative design. Its greatest failure is not what it regulates, but what it prevents from ever existing within the U.S. market. By closing the door on stock-based and derivative-based stablecoins, the Act has ensured that the U.S. will be a follower, not a leader, in a crucial area of digital finance, and this may be its most enduring and damaging legacy.

Chapter 13: Stablecoin 1.4- Forcing Digital Asset Packs Off-Shore

“It is a way to take people’s wealth from them without having to openly raise taxes. Inflation is the most universal tax of all.”

Thomas Sowell[16]

The GENIUS Act’s most significant failing may not be what it explicitly bans, but what it strategically excludes. This is a subtle but potent form of regulatory control, a type of "definitional iron cage" that traps stablecoin innovation within the narrow confines of traditional financial assets. This chapter focuses on Stablecoin 1.4, a category of tokens whose value is derived from or backed by a basket of diverse digital assets. The Act's provisions, while ostensibly designed to ensure stability and consumer protection, are meticulously crafted to render these tokens non-compliant, forcing their development and usage to the more accommodating shores of other nations. As Thomas Sowell once observed, “Inflation is the most universal tax of all,” and the GENIUS Act's singular focus on fiat-backed tokens leaves stablecoin users entirely exposed to this tax, while simultaneously exiling the very innovations that could offer a hedge against it.

[16] Staff (2025). “Inflation Quotes.” Brainy Quote at https://www.brainyquote.com/topics/inflation-quotes.

The Act's methodology is a direct consequence of a fundamental distrust of crypto-native stability mechanisms. Instead of creating a framework that could harness the power of on-chain collateral and decentralized governance, the GENIUS Act mandates a centralized, off-chain, and fiat-based model. This approach is not a regulatory oversight; it is a strategic choice to preserve the legacy financial system by defining "safety" in terms of traditional, government-backed assets. Stablecoins backed by a basket of digital assets represent a parallel financial system, a form of value that is transparently collateralized on-chain and not beholden to the monetary policies of a single nation. It is this independence that makes them a threat, and it is this independence that the GENIUS Act works so diligently to subvert.

The iron cage of the GENIUS Act begins with its narrow and exclusive definitions. By defining a "payment stablecoin" and "High-Quality Liquid Assets" (HQLAs) in a way that includes only fiat currency and short-term Treasuries, the Act creates an insurmountable barrier for any stablecoin whose stability is derived from a diverse basket of digital assets. Even if such a token were significantly over-collateralized with assets like Bitcoin or Ethereum, the Act simply does not recognize these as legitimate reserves. The consequence is a regulatory "brick wall" that makes domestic operation impossible for these models, leaving them with no choice but to exist and thrive in other, more permissive jurisdictions.

Ultimately, this policy choice is a self-inflicted wound for the U.S. as a global leader in finance and technology. By preemptively banning a category of innovation that has already shown promise—with examples like DAI demonstrating resilience across market cycles—the Act closes the door on a more robust and resilient future for digital assets. It cedes market share, talent, and regulatory influence to nations willing to explore these concepts. The offshore exodus of these projects is not a side effect of the GENIUS Act; it is the inevitable and, by all appearances, intended outcome of a regulatory framework that prioritizes the old over the new, and a centralized system over a decentralized one.

The Definitional Iron Cage: Excluding Digital Asset Baskets

The GENIUS Act's stringent definition of a "payment stablecoin" and its exclusive list of permissible reserves act as an impenetrable barrier for stablecoins backed by a basket of diverse digital assets. By mandating that such stablecoins be redeemable for a fixed monetary value and backed by an extremely narrow list of "High-Quality Liquid Assets" (HQLAs)—including U.S. currency and short-term Treasuries—the Act fundamentally excludes any token whose value is derived from a mix of cryptocurrencies. Even if a basket of assets like Bitcoin and Ethereum were to provide significant over-collateralization, the Act simply doesn't recognize these assets as valid reserves. This creates a regulatory brick wall, forcing these promising models to operate outside the U.S. and preventing a vital area of innovation from taking root domestically.

Furthermore, the Act's incompatibility with decentralized and algorithmically-enhanced stability mechanisms also pushes these models offshore. Many digital asset-backed stablecoins leverage smart contracts and decentralized governance, often through a DAO, to maintain their peg. However, the GENIUS Act requires a centralized "Permitted Payment Stablecoin Issuer" (PPSI) with explicit legal obligations and the technical capability to "seize, freeze, or burn" tokens. This mandate for a centralized, accountable entity with powers of intervention directly contradicts the core principles of decentralization inherent in projects like Dai (DAI). DAI, arguably the most prominent example of a crypto-collateralized stablecoin, has maintained its peg through a decentralized protocol, a model that is entirely incompatible with the GENIUS Act's framework, thus ensuring its continued development and use remains outside U.S. jurisdiction.

Overlooking Unique Strengths and Resilience of Digital Asset Baskets

The GENIUS Act's focus on fiat-backed stablecoins completely overlooks the potential for diversification and resilience offered by digital asset baskets. Fiat-backed stablecoins are inherently tied to the monetary policy and economic health of a single nation's currency, making them vulnerable to inflation and

Quantitative Easing (QE). In contrast, stablecoins backed by a diversified basket of uncorrelated digital assets could offer a valuable hedge against these specific risks, aiming for true purchasing power stability rather than just nominal dollar stability. By mandating exposure to U.S. dollar inflation, the Act stifles the development of these more resilient models, pushing them to operate in jurisdictions that recognize the value of diversification.

Another key strength that is overlooked is the inherent transparency and auditability of on-chain collateral. While fiat-backed stablecoins rely on external attestations and bank audits, which can sometimes be opaque or delayed, crypto-backed stablecoins often maintain their collateral on-chain, visible and auditable by anyone. The Act, however, disregards this key advantage. Instead of creating a regulatory framework that leverages the inherent transparency of on-chain collateral, it disallows such collateral altogether for "payment stablecoins." This dismissal of a core benefit of crypto-native design ensures that these innovative projects are developed in jurisdictions that embrace on-chain transparency as a feature, not a bug.

The Act's approach also suffers from a regulatory presumption of risk, rather than a nuanced assessment of different models. While the collapse of Terra/Luna highlighted the dangers of some algorithmic designs, other crypto-collateralized stablecoins, like DAI, have demonstrated remarkable resilience for years through multiple market cycles. Yet, the GENIUS Act applies a broad-stroke condemnation of all non-fiat-backed stability mechanisms. This lack of nuance and the presumptive judgment of risk effectively foreclose any legitimate crypto-native stablecoin from operating domestically, forcing projects with robust and innovative designs to seek regulatory clarity and market acceptance elsewhere.

The Offshore Exodus of Innovation and Market Share

The GENIUS Act's narrow regulatory environment creates a powerful incentive for innovators, developers, and entrepreneurs to take their projects elsewhere. By making it impossible for digital asset-backed stablecoins to operate in the U.S., the Act directly encourages the establishment and growth of these projects in countries with more accommodating regulatory stances. This results in a "brain drain" and "capital flight" away from the U.S., ceding innovation and market share to global competitors and undermining the U.S.'s goal of becoming a leader in the digital asset space.

This creates a fragmented global stablecoin market and encourages regulatory arbitrage. Non-compliant digital asset-backed stablecoins will continue to exist and be traded globally, but primarily outside the direct purview of U.S. regulation. U.S. users who want to access these alternatives will be forced to engage with offshore, less-regulated platforms. This outcome ironically increases their exposure to risk, undermining the very protective aims of the GENIUS Act and creating a more dangerous environment for consumers who are forced to operate in the shadows to access the financial products they desire.

The Act also ensures that the U.S. will not be a leader in advanced digital asset concepts. The future of digital finance might involve dynamic basket stablecoins that automatically rebalance, or sophisticated crypto-native collateralized debt positions. By effectively banning these now, the GENIUS Act guarantees the U.S. will be a follower, not a developer, of these potentially advanced forms of digital money. This relinquishes America's claim as a "cryptocurrency capital of the world," leaving it with a role limited to the tokenization of simple fiat currencies.

Conclusion

The GENIUS Act's handling of digital asset-backed stablecoins is a defining moment for U.S. financial regulation, revealing a deliberate choice to prioritize the preservation of traditional financial structures over the embrace of genuine innovation. By creating a regulatory framework that acts as a definitive iron cage, the Act systematically excludes Stablecoin 1.4—tokens backed by baskets of diverse digital assets. The narrow definitions of "payment stablecoin" and "High-Quality Liquid Assets" are not accidents; they are strategic choices that render any crypto-native collateral structure non-compliant, forcing this crucial area of innovation off-shore.

A key consequence of this policy is the outright dismissal of the unique strengths and resilience offered by digital asset-backed models. These stablecoins offer a form of diversification that can hedge against the inherent risks of a single fiat currency, such as inflation and central bank monetary policy. Furthermore, their on-chain collateral provides a level of transparency and auditability that, in many cases, surpasses traditional off-chain attestations. By ignoring these benefits, the Act reveals a profound lack of foresight, choosing to reinforce the status quo rather than build a more robust and resilient financial future based on crypto-native principles.

The most damaging legacy of this approach is the offshore exodus of talent, innovation, and market share. By making it impossible for projects like DAI to operate domestically, the U.S. is signaling to the world that its regulatory environment is hostile to the most creative and ambitious ideas in the digital asset space. This "brain drain" and "capital flight" is a direct result of the Act's rigid, non-negotiable terms, which have created a stark divide between what is legally permissible in the U.S. and what is technically and economically viable in the global crypto market.

The Act's flawed assumption is that all non-fiat-backed stablecoins are inherently too risky, a judgment that ignores years of data and the proven resilience of models like DAI. This broad-stroke condemnation, rather than a nuanced assessment of different designs, not only stifles domestic innovation but also ironically exposes U.S. consumers to greater risk by forcing them to interact with less-regulated, offshore platforms. The Act's protective aims are, therefore, undermined by its own inflexibility, creating a more dangerous environment for the very people it purports to protect.

In conclusion, the GENIUS Act's handling of stablecoin 1.4 is a strategic misstep with long-term consequences. It is a piece of legislation that has effectively banned a category of financial innovation that could offer a genuine hedge against the vulnerabilities of fiat currency. By forcing digital asset basket tokens off-shore, the Act has ensured that the U.S. will be a follower, not a leader, in a crucial area of digital finance, cementing a reputation as a country that prioritizes political compromise and legacy systems over the promise of a more innovative and resilient financial future.

Chapter 14: Stablecoin 1.7 & 1.9-The Curse of Rothchild: The Assault on Land and Commodity Based Tokens

"Every regulatory speech on derivatives takes a bow to their hedging 'benefits.' Less publically, regulators pay their respects to derivative profits, a blessed relief from their banks' troubled loans to less developed countries, highly leveraged companies, and real estate swingers."

Carol Loomis[17]

The GENIUS Act, presented as a framework for stabilizing digital assets, functions more like a Trojan horse, concealing a strategic assault on land and commodity-based tokens—Stablecoin 1.7 and 1.9. This legislation does not simply regulate; it actively curates the digital economy, ensuring that its foundational layer remains inextricably linked to the debt-based fiat system. In doing so, the Act denies the possibility of a "merit-based" financial system where value is derived from productive assets rather than from government liabilities. The consequence is a digital financial landscape that is not a departure from the old but merely a digitized extension of it, perpetuating the very vulnerabilities crypto was designed to transcend.

[17] Staff (2025). "Regulatory Quotes." Brainy Quote at https://www.brainyquote.com/topics/regulatory-quotes.

This assault is best understood through the lens of the "Rothschild System" analogy, a critique of traditional finance that posits it is fundamentally built on debt creation. Banks create money through lending, and governments issue bonds that are often monetized by central banks, creating an ever-expanding cycle of debt. By mandating that compliant stablecoins be backed exclusively by U.S. fiat currency or short-term Treasuries, the GENIUS Act digitizes and legitimizes this exact mechanism. It ensures that the digital dollar, the central building block of the new economy, is not a new form of value but a reinforced link in the chain of government debt.

The Act's exclusion of other forms of collateral is not an oversight; it is a deliberate and calculated choice. Stablecoins backed by a transparent and verifiable basket of non-debt assets—such as land, commodities, or equities—could offer a new form of digital savings. These models, like Stablecoin 1.7 (real-world asset baskets) and 1.9 (single asset classes), could provide a hedge against the inflationary pressures of fiat currency. Yet, the GENIUS Act explicitly disallows such a development, forcing users to accept fiat's inherent vulnerabilities. It is a regulatory move that prevents the emergence of true alternatives, solidifying the monopoly of the debt-based system.

Further entrenching this paradigm is the Act's "no yield" prohibition. By banning Permitted Payment Stablecoin Issuers (PPSIs) from paying interest or yield, the Act effectively turns stablecoins into non-productive digital cash equivalents. This is a direct attack on the concept of merit-based finance, where capital is expected to earn a return based on its productive use or the value of its underlying collateral. This prohibition disincentivizes genuine digital savings and forces capital seeking a return back into the very traditional debt instruments—like bank deposits and bonds—that the Act champions, thereby reinforcing the existing system's characteristics.

This legislation also serves to consolidate control within the hands of existing financial power structures. By limiting stablecoin issuance to highly regulated and well-capitalized institutions, the GENIUS Act prevents the emergence of decentralized, grassroots, or "merit-based" models. Instead of fostering competition from new, potentially more efficient, and transparent protocols, it entrenches the power of traditional banks, ensuring they remain the gatekeepers of digital value. As Carol Loomis noted of derivatives, regulatory speeches may pay lip service to "hedging 'benefits,'" but less publicly, regulators often respect the profits and power of the established financial players.

The consequence for the end-user is a lack of hedge against the very real risks of fiscal and monetary policy. Stablecoins locked to fiat or government debt are directly exposed to the risks of government fiscal irresponsibility and central bank decisions like quantitative easing. A stablecoin truly backed by land or commodities could, theoretically, offer a more resilient store of value by divorcing itself from political and economic whims. The GENIUS Act denies this choice, effectively forcing users to absorb the risks inherent in the very debt-based financial system it reinforces.

In sum, this chapter will deconstruct the GENIUS Act's provisions to reveal its true nature: a legislative instrument that crushes the vision of a parallel, asset-backed financial system. By examining its core tenets—the exclusive backing by debt instruments, the prohibition on yield, and the centralization of control—it becomes clear that the Act is not a neutral framework but a deliberate and strategic effort to preserve the existing order, thereby ensuring that digital money, in the U.S. at least, remains firmly under the curse of debt-based finance.

Entrenching Debt-Based Fiat and Government Bonds as the Sole Foundation

The GENIUS Act's most direct assault on alternative stablecoins is its explicit entrenchment of debt-based finance as the sole foundation for digital money. By strictly limiting the backing of "payment stablecoins" to U.S. fiat currency or short-term U.S. Treasury securities, the Act creates a monopoly for government liabilities. Fiat currency is a liability of the central bank, and government bonds are explicit debt instruments. This is the heart of the "Rothschild System" analogy, where a financial order is built upon the continuous creation of debt. The GENIUS Act doesn't challenge this system; it digitally reinforces it, extending its reach into the world of cryptocurrency and ensuring that the fundamental building blocks of digital money are a reflection of this debt-based paradigm.

This legislation also works to disable any alternative stablecoin models that could bypass central bank debt. The Act's exclusion of other collateral forms, such as diversified baskets of real-world assets (Stablecoin 1.7) or single-asset-class tokens (Stablecoin 1.9), is a deliberate choice to prevent stablecoins from being backed by productive assets. Stablecoins genuinely backed by transparent and verifiable assets like gold, energy, or real estate could offer a form of digital savings that is not directly exposed to the inflationary pressures of fiat currency or the risks of government debt. The GENIUS Act explicitly disallows such "asset-backed" digital currencies from gaining widespread use, forcing individuals to accept the inherent vulnerabilities of a fiat system and its accompanying debt-based structure.

Breaking Down Merit-Based Finance and True Savings Mechanisms

The GENIUS Act's assault on alternative models is further cemented by its prohibition on yield. By banning Permitted Payment Stablecoin Issuers (PPSIs) from paying interest or yield, the Act turns compliant stablecoins into non-productive digital cash equivalents, mirroring physical cash whose purchasing power erodes with inflation. This provision directly works against a "merit-based" financial system, where capital is expected to earn a return based on its productive use or the underlying value of its collateral. By disincentivizing digital savings within the compliant ecosystem, the Act forces capital seeking yield back into traditional debt instruments, thereby ensuring that the existing system of credit and debt remains the primary engine of finance.

This "no yield" rule also fundamentally crushes the vision of a new form of digital savings. Many in the crypto space envision digital assets as a way to "opt out" of the traditional debt-based financial system, offering alternatives that prioritize individual sovereignty and transparent ownership of assets. This vision includes the ability for capital to generate returns based on the merit of a protocol or the value of real-world backing, rather than being intermediated through debt. The GENIUS Act, however, prevents this from becoming a reality for stablecoins in the U.S. Instead of enabling a new form of digital savings, it forces stablecoins to become an extension of the existing system's liabilities, thereby reinforcing its propensity for inflation and debt expansion.

Consolidation, Control, and the Perpetuation of Existing Power Structures

By limiting stablecoin issuance to a select group of highly regulated, well-capitalized financial institutions, the GENIUS Act centralizes control over digital money. This aligns perfectly with a system where powerful, established entities are the gatekeepers of finance. This consolidation of power prevents the decentralized, grassroots, or "merit-based" emergence of alternative stablecoin models. Rather than fostering competition from new, potentially more efficient or transparent models, the Act entrenches the power of existing financial institutions, much as traditional banks have historically dominated the creation and distribution of debt-based money, thereby perpetuating existing power structures.

Stablecoins locked to fiat or government debt are directly exposed to the risks of government fiscal and monetary policy. This includes the risk of excessive government spending leading to inflation or central bank policies that devalue the currency. A "merit-based" or truly asset-backed stablecoin—like one tied to commodities or real estate—could, theoretically, offer a more resilient store of value by divorcing itself from the political and economic decisions that influence fiat. The GENIUS Act denies this hedge to U.S. stablecoin users, forcing them to absorb the risks inherent in the very debt-based financial system it reinforces.

The philosophical underpinning of much of crypto is the creation of a parallel financial system that offers alternatives to traditional finance's debt-centric nature. The GENIUS Act directly hinders this vision. By subsuming stablecoins entirely into the existing regulatory and asset-backing framework, the Act prevents them from being a genuine stepping stone toward a truly alternative, asset-backed, or merit-based financial future within the U.S. Instead, compliant stablecoins become merely a more efficient interface for the existing debt-based system, rather than a departure from it.

Conclusion

The GENIUS Act's assault on Stablecoin 1.7 and 1.9 reveals a profound strategic choice: to preserve and digitize the traditional debt-based financial system rather than allow for the emergence of genuine alternatives. By creating an ironclad monopoly for fiat and government debt as the only acceptable collateral for stablecoins, the Act has ensured that the foundational layer of digital money in the U.S. remains under the "Curse of Rothschild"—a system where value is generated not from productive assets but from government liabilities and credit expansion.

This legislative framework is not a neutral regulator; it is a tool of entrenchment. By explicitly disallowing stablecoins backed by real-world assets like land or commodities, and by prohibiting any form of yield, the Act systematically breaks down the possibility of "merit-based finance" within its jurisdiction. It forces capital to seek returns through the traditional debt paradigm, preventing the development of a digital savings mechanism that could offer a true hedge against the inflationary pressures of fiat currency.

The true consequence of this policy is a consolidation of power. The Act centralizes control in the hands of existing, well-capitalized financial institutions and ensures they remain the gatekeepers of digital value. This prevents a decentralized, grassroots emergence of new financial models and reinforces the dominance of a system where banks and government-issued debt are the non-negotiable cornerstones. The "benefits" of this regulation, as Carol Loomis might suggest, are a public facade that obscures the real goal: protecting the profits and perpetuating the power of the established financial players.

In essence, the GENIUS Act ensures that stablecoins in the U.S. will not be a revolutionary new form of money, but rather a more efficient, digital extension of the old system. It denies citizens a crucial hedge against the risks of fiscal and monetary policy, forcing them to absorb the vulnerabilities inherent in a debt-centric economy. This is a monumental missed opportunity to foster a more resilient, transparent, and independent financial future.

Ultimately, the GENIUS Act will be remembered not for what it enabled, but for what it prevented. It is a piece of legislation that has solidified the debt-based paradigm in the digital realm and, in doing so, has cemented its legacy as a protector of the status quo rather than a facilitator of genuine innovation.

Chapter 15: The Death of Better Money-Attacking the Idea of Stablecoin 2.0 and Beyond

"The efficiency, credibility, and liquidity of the financial markets have been foundational to the largest economy in the world."

Dan Gilbert.[18]

The quote from Dan Gilbert is a potent reminder of the foundation of economic prosperity. In the digital age, this principle extends to stablecoins—digital assets that promise a stable value and are seen as a critical bridge between the traditional financial system and the decentralized future. Stablecoins offer the speed, transparency, and global reach of blockchain technology while mitigating the extreme volatility of traditional cryptocurrencies like Bitcoin. However, the promise of stablecoins has always been twofold: to create a digital version of existing money and to create a better version of money that addresses the inherent flaws of fiat currency.

This chapter argues that the GENIUS Act, a landmark piece of legislation aimed at regulating payment stablecoins in the United States, effectively destroys the possibility of creating "better money." While the Act provides a clear regulatory framework for the first category of stablecoins—what we might call

[18] Staff (2025). "Liquidity Quotes" Brainy Quote at https://www.brainyquote.com/topics/liquidity-quotes.

Stablecoin 1.0 (and its iterations)—it fundamentally attacks the very idea of Stablecoin 2.0 and the innovations that lie beyond. In its attempt to provide stability and security, the legislation paradoxically stifles the exact kind of innovation needed to truly improve the financial system for the digital era.

The core problem lies in the Act's rigid, fiat-centric mindset. It defines a compliant "payment stablecoin" as one backed 1:1 by U.S. dollars and short-term U.S. Treasury securities. This is a classic Stablecoin 1.0 approach: a digital dollar, plain and simple. While this may offer nominal stability, it does nothing to address the elephant in the room—the U.S. dollar's own purchasing power is constantly eroding due to inflation and is subject to the unpredictable whims of central bank monetary policy. The Act, therefore, forces compliant stablecoins to inherit all the flaws of the very system they could be designed to improve upon.

Consequently, the GENIUS Act launches a direct assault on "smart money" concepts. One of the most promising ideas, the "basket of goods" theory, seeks to peg a stablecoin's value not to a single fiat currency but to a diverse index of real-world commodities and consumer goods. This would create a system designed to maintain real purchasing power, offering a genuine hedge against inflation. In addition, the Act's prohibition on yield-bearing and smart burn technology prevents the development of advanced, crypto-native mechanisms that could enhance stability, create deflationary pressure, and offer a productive store of value.

Ultimately, the GENIUS Act creates a regulatory environment that eliminates any competition for traditional fiat and drives "smart money" innovation offshore. By restricting compliant stablecoins to a conservative, non-productive model, the U.S. risks ceding its leadership in the most cutting-edge areas of digital monetary development. The Act is a shortsighted piece of legislation that misses the opportunity to position the U.S. at the forefront of digital financial evolution. The remainder of this chapter will delve into these specific legislative provisions and explain how they, in effect, are killing the future of "better money."

Killing "Stablecoin 2.0" and the Basket of Goods Theory

The GENIUS Act's most significant failing is its rigid, fiat-centric straightjacket, which requires "payment stablecoins" to be backed 1:1 by U.S. dollars and short-term U.S. Treasury securities. This policy rigidly defines stability in terms of nominal dollar value, fundamentally misunderstanding or dismissing innovative "smart money" concepts that aim for real purchasing power stability. For example, a "basket of goods" stablecoin would peg its value to a diverse index of real-world commodities or consumer goods. This would create a counter-inflationary system where the stablecoin's value adjusts to maintain purchasing power even as fiat currency inflates. By making such a design impossible for a compliant "payment stablecoin," the GENIUS Act stifles a key avenue for innovation.

By exclusively linking payment stablecoins to the U.S. dollar, the GENIUS Act forces digital money to inherit all the vulnerabilities of fiat currency. This includes the consistent erosion of purchasing power due to inflation, the devaluation effects of central bank actions like Quantitative Easing (QE), and the susceptibility to political manipulation. A stablecoin tied to the dollar is only "stable" in nominal terms and is inherently unstable in real purchasing power over time. The Act effectively forces digital money to inherit these flaws, thereby preventing the development of truly resilient, counter-inflationary digital assets that could offer a genuine hedge against fiat's inherent weaknesses.

Prohibiting Yield-Bearing and Smart Burn Technology for Payment Tokens

A critical provision of the GENIUS Act is its blanket prohibition on Permitted Payment Stablecoin Issuers (PPSIs) offering any interest or yield to stablecoin holders. This directly attacks innovative "smart money" designs that could bake yield generation into a stablecoin's mechanics to help offset inflation. By forcing "payment stablecoins" to be non-productive assets, unlike even traditional savings accounts, the Act discourages long-term holding and savings within the digital asset ecosystem. This legislative choice pushes capital back into traditional, debt-based financial products and prevents digital money from becoming a more useful and productive form of a store of value.

The Act also suppresses "smart burn" technology and other ecosystem-enhancing mechanisms. Smart burn is an advanced, crypto-native feature where a portion of transaction fees is programmatically used to buy underlying assets into the stablecoin's ecosystem, enhancing its stability and creating deflationary pressure. However, the GENIUS Act's strict "payment token" definition and "no yield" rule make such sophisticated, self-sustaining mechanisms fundamentally incompatible with its regulatory framework. If the "burn" mechanism benefits holders, it could be construed as an impermissible yield or an investment-like activity, which the Act seeks to prevent. This eliminates a powerful tool for creating a truly stable and anti-inflationary digital asset system.

Stifling Innovation and Driving "Smart Money" Offshore

By ensuring that only fiat-backed, non-yield-bearing stablecoins can operate compliantly, the GENIUS Act effectively eliminates any competition from "Stablecoin 2.0" designs that could offer superior properties like inflation resistance or integrated yield. This protects the traditional fiat system from digital disruption and limits the choices available to consumers and businesses. It forces the market to accept a "digital dollar" that behaves just like its physical counterpart, complete with its inherent weaknesses, thus preventing the market from discovering genuinely superior forms of digital money.

The prohibition on "smart money" designs also creates a significant risk of brain drain and offshore innovation. By discouraging developers and entrepreneurs from pursuing projects with yield-bearing or advanced algorithmic components, the Act incentivizes them to seek more accommodating regulatory environments. The U.S. risks ceding leadership in the most cutting-edge areas of stablecoin development, forcing the "smart money" innovation that could address fiat's vulnerabilities to flourish elsewhere. This could ultimately create a future where U.S. citizens and businesses rely on foreign-issued, more advanced digital assets for their financial needs.

The long-term damage to U.S. competitiveness is a critical concern. The GENIUS Act's conservative, "386-era" stablecoin model prevents the U.S. from positioning itself at the forefront of digital monetary evolution. In an increasingly digital and volatile global economy, the ability to create and manage truly "smart money" that offers resilience beyond simple fiat pegs could be a significant strategic advantage. The Act's limitations mean the U.S. is not actively supporting the development of stablecoins that could offer superior value preservation or financial utility in the face of ongoing inflation and unpredictable monetary policies. This shortsightedness could ultimately weaken the U.S.'s long-term economic and financial leadership in the digital age.

Conclusion

The GENIUS Act, while lauded for providing a clear regulatory framework for stablecoins, represents a significant setback for the future of digital money. In its attempt to instill a sense of security and stability, the legislation has adopted a deeply flawed, fiat-centric mindset that effectively kills off the most promising innovations in the space. The act's rigid definition of a stablecoin, tied exclusively to the nominal value of the U.S. dollar, prevents the development of "smart money" designs like the basket of goods theory. This approach, while seemingly prudent, fundamentally ignores the inherent instability of the fiat system itself—namely, the constant erosion of purchasing power due to inflation.

This legislative assault extends beyond the basic definition of stability to the very mechanics of a stablecoin's operation. By prohibiting yield-bearing mechanisms, the GENIUS Act prevents stablecoins from becoming productive, inflation-resistant assets. This is a critical blow to financial innovation, as it forces digital assets to remain non-productive, unlike traditional savings accounts or other financial instruments that generate returns. It also effectively bans "smart burn" technology, a powerful, crypto-native tool that could programmatically enhance a stablecoin's stability and backing. These prohibitions are not just minor restrictions; they are fundamental attacks on the core principles of creating a truly resilient and value-preserving form of digital money.

The consequences of this approach are far-reaching and potentially devastating for U.S. competitiveness. By eliminating any compliant competition from innovative "Stablecoin 2.0" designs, the GENIUS Act protects the traditional fiat system from digital disruption and limits the choices available to consumers and businesses. It ensures that the only viable "digital dollar" is one that behaves exactly like its physical counterpart, complete with its inherent weaknesses. This policy prevents the natural market discovery of superior financial products and cements a conservative approach that stifles progress in one of the most dynamic sectors of finance.

Perhaps the most significant long-term risk of the GENIUS Act is the inevitable brain drain and offshore flight of innovation it will provoke. Entrepreneurs, developers, and innovators with ambitious plans for more sophisticated stablecoins—those with yield-bearing or algorithmic components—will be forced to pursue their projects in jurisdictions with more accommodating regulatory environments. The U.S. is effectively ceding its leadership in digital monetary evolution to other nations, creating a future where its citizens may be reliant on foreign-issued, more advanced digital assets. This is a strategic misstep that could weaken the U.S.'s position in the global digital economy.

In conclusion, the GENIUS Act is not a triumph of regulatory clarity but an act of regulatory self-sabotage. Instead of embracing the opportunity to develop truly "better money" that can offer resilience and value preservation in the face of ongoing inflation and unpredictable monetary policies, the Act doubles down on a conservative model. This approach protects the status quo at the expense of progress, innovation, and long-term economic leadership. For the U.S. to truly thrive in the digital age, it must move beyond the fiat-centric straightjacket and create a regulatory environment that fosters, rather than fears, the next generation of "smart money."

PART III: Building The Future for ABT

Chapter 16: The ABT Terminology Change

"Our liquidity is fine. As a matter of fact, it's better than fine. It's strong."

Kenneth Lay[19]

The power of legislation often lies not just in its explicit rules, but in the subtle shifts in language and terminology it introduces. The GENIUS Act, in its effort to regulate the burgeoning digital asset space, serves as a prime example of this phenomenon. By meticulously defining and categorizing certain assets, the Act subtly steers the entire ecosystem towards a specific vision of digital money while simultaneously marginalizing others. The seemingly neutral act of standardizing terminology for "payment stablecoins" and "asset-backed tokens" is, in reality, a powerful legislative tool designed to shape the market and protect incumbent interests.

At the heart of the Act's new lexicon is a fundamental bias. The legislation heavily favors a narrow definition of "payment stablecoin" that requires rigid backing by a select group of High-Quality Liquid Assets, primarily U.S. dollars and short-term Treasuries. This approach implicitly re-frames all other innovative digital asset designs—such as those backed by diverse digital or real-world assets—as non-compliant or relegated to

[19] Staff (2025). "Liquidity Quotes." Brainy Quote at https://www.brainyquote.com/topics/liquidity-quotes.

an undefined regulatory abyss. The Act is not creating a level playing field for all forms of digital money; instead, it is building a linguistic fence that forces the market to conform to a single, pre-approved model.

This semantic manipulation is a prelude to the chapter's central argument: the profound hypocrisy embedded within the GENIUS Act's reserve requirements. The legislation imposes an extraordinary burden on new digital forms of money, demanding a level of prudence and financial backing that is completely absent from the very institutions the Act is seemingly designed to buttress. This double standard is more than a mere inconsistency; it reveals a deep-seated bias against digital innovation and a protective impulse towards the existing, debt-based financial order.

The stark contrast is laid bare in the Act's punitive approach to reserves. While the new digital money is mandated to have 100% backing by specific, highly liquid assets, the traditional banking sector operates on a fundamentally different principle. For years, major commercial banks have leveraged a **fractional reserve system**, and in many cases, have had a 0% reserve requirement on checking deposits. This disparity creates a world where the legacy system is allowed to operate with virtually no backing, while its potential digital successor is subjected to the strictest possible prudential standards.

This chapter will delve into this hypocrisy, demonstrating how the GENIUS Act’s terminology change and its stringent reserve requirements are not about consumer protection but about **solidifying the reign of existing powers.** It will show how the Act codifies the limited "On-Ramp/Off-Ramp" model of digital money, stifles more resilient "smart money" innovations, and ultimately creates a two-tiered global market where the U.S. is left with a safe but stagnant form of digital finance.

The New Terminology: "Asset-Backed Tokens" and Their Implicit Disadvantage

The GENIUS Act introduces a specific and restrictive terminology for "payment stablecoins," defining them by their redemption obligation to a fixed monetary value and their backing by High-Quality Liquid Assets (HQLAs) like fiat and short-term Treasuries. While the term "asset-backed token" might be used more broadly in crypto discourse for tokens representing anything from real estate to gold, the context of the GENIUS Act's definition heavily biases the entire category towards fiat/Treasury backing. This legislative choice effectively pushes other forms of asset-backed tokens—for example, those backed by a 50% reserve of diverse digital assets or real-world non-HQLA assets—into a non-compliant or undefined regulatory grey area for use as "payment tokens." The Act's strict demand for 100% backing by specific HQLAs creates a "50% backing" trap, where any token designed to maintain stability with less than 100% is immediately excluded from the "payment stablecoin" category, thereby stifling many innovative asset-backed digital designs.

The Contrast with Major Banks (0% Backing)

A powerful critique of the GENIUS Act's stringency on digital assets is its stark contrast with the fractional reserve banking system. Traditional commercial banks operate on a fractional reserve system, effectively creating money through lending with reserves far less than 100%. In some jurisdictions, this has even been a 0% reserve requirement for checking deposits. This double standard is a glaring example of regulatory bias. The Act demands 100% HQLA backing for stablecoin issuers, a bar far higher than what is expected of the traditional banks that underpin the existing "debt-based finance" system. This "0% backing" for major banks, relative to the 100% for stablecoins, paints the Act as a protective measure for incumbent financial powers. The hypocrisy is palpable, as the legislation imposes the strictest possible standards on new entrants while allowing existing players to operate with minimal constraints.

Solidifying the Reign of "OROR Tokens" (Tether/Circle's Model)

The GENIUS Act's requirements—1:1 fiat/Treasury backing, centralized issuance, regulatory oversight, and the ability to "seize, freeze, or burn"—perfectly describe the operational models of major fiat-backed stablecoin issuers like Tether (USDT) and Circle

(USDC). These tokens primarily serve as direct digital representations of the U.S. dollar, facilitating transfers into and out of the broader crypto ecosystem. The pejorative term "OROR Tokens" (On-Ramp/Off-Ramp Tokens) captures the critical sentiment that these stablecoins are merely digital conduits for fiat, lacking true innovation beyond basic tokenization. They act as "blockchain versions of a debit card" because their utility is largely confined to moving fiat value on a blockchain, without the inherent improvements to monetary policy or inflation hedging that proponents of decentralized finance envision. The Act solidifies this limited role, mandating that this "extra steps" model is the only permissible one.

Exclusion of Counter-Inflationary Mechanisms

By forcing stablecoins to be 1:1 backed by fiat, the Act inherently ties their long-term value to the purchasing power erosion of the underlying currency due to inflation and quantitative easing. This legislative decision prevents the emergence of "smart money" designed as a hedge against inflation, such as those backed by a basket of real goods or dynamically adjusted based on inflation metrics. The Act's framework ensures that the "payment stablecoin" remains a subservient digital proxy for a depreciating fiat, rather than an independent, more resilient form of digital value. This makes "OROR Tokens" the only game in town, even if their underlying fiat has fundamental weaknesses, effectively preventing the evolution of truly innovative and resilient digital assets.

Suppressing Diverse Collateralization and Centralizing Control

The Act's strict reserve requirements shut down experimentation with various collateral types and sophisticated risk management models that could offer unique benefits. For instance, a stablecoin over-collateralized with a diverse set of digital assets, managed by a decentralized autonomous organization (DAO) with transparent on-chain governance, might be viewed by some as a more robust and innovative system than a centralized entity holding off-chain fiat. However, the Act's insistence on centralized Permitted Payment Stablecoin Issuers (PPSIs) with "kill switch" capabilities centralizes control over these digital assets. This is antithetical to the decentralized ethos of much of the crypto community and further reinforces the "OROR Token" paradigm where a central issuer maintains ultimate authority, ensuring that control remains in the hands of a few gatekeepers.

Disincentivizing True Asset Tokenization for Payments

While the broader term "asset-backed tokens" exists, the Act's regulatory requirements make it impractical for tokens truly representing ownership of a diverse set of real-world assets (e.g., a diversified portfolio of tokenized stocks, real estate, or commodities) to function as "payment stablecoins" in the U.S. This limits the tokenization revolution to primarily representing fiat currency, preventing the broader vision where everyday payments could be seamlessly conducted with tokens directly representing productive assets or more stable measures of value. The "OROR Token" status remains entrenched, hindering the integration of real-world assets into the payment layer and restricting the utility of digital assets to a narrow, fiat-adjacent function.

Offshore Exodus and the Bifurcation of the Crypto Market

The regulatory clarity provided by the GENIUS Act primarily benefits the "OROR Token" model, creating a clear and safe path for them. However, any stablecoin project that aims for true decentralization, diverse asset backing (beyond fiat/Treasuries), or counter-inflationary mechanisms will find no viable path in the U.S. and will be compelled to move offshore. This creates a bifurcated global market: a highly regulated, "safe," but innovation-constrained "OROR Token" market in the U.S., and a more experimental, diverse, but potentially riskier market operating in less regulated jurisdictions. This undermines America's potential to lead the entire spectrum of stablecoin innovation and cedes a crucial area of financial technology to foreign competitors.

Conclusion

The GENIUS Act's subtle but impactful terminology changes for "payment stablecoins" are not a benign act of regulatory standardization; they are a calculated move to reinforce a specific, limited vision of digital money. By demanding that all compliant stablecoins be backed 1:1 by U.S. dollars and short-term Treasuries, the Act effectively legislates the end of "smart money" innovation and solidifies the dominance of a few centralized issuers. The most damning aspect of this entire framework, however, is the profound hypocrisy it embodies.

The hypocrisy is undeniable. The Act places a suffocating 100% reserve requirement on new, digital forms of money while simultaneously allowing the traditional banking system to operate on a fractional reserve basis—in many cases, with a 0% reserve requirement. This is not a level playing field. It is a legislative moat designed to protect the legacy financial system from true digital disruption, ensuring that the new digital money cannot outperform its traditional counterpart in terms of resilience and capital efficiency. This double standard exposes the Act as a protective measure for incumbent financial institutions rather than a genuine effort to foster a secure and innovative digital financial ecosystem.

Furthermore, the Act's strict requirements ensure that only the limited “On-Ramp/Off-Ramp” model of stablecoins, epitomized by Tether and Circle, can thrive. By mandating that compliant stablecoins are merely digital conduits for fiat and prohibiting counter-inflationary mechanisms, the legislation deliberately ties the fate of digital money to the inherent weaknesses of the depreciating fiat currency it represents. This strategic decision prevents the emergence of stablecoins designed to be resilient stores of value, like those backed by a basket of goods, and forces the market to accept a subservient digital proxy rather than a genuinely better form of money.

The Act's centralization of control is another critical failure. By mandating centralized issuers with "kill switch" capabilities and stifling experimentation with diverse collateral and decentralized governance models, the legislation directly opposes the core ethos of many in the crypto community. This not only discourages innovation but also consolidates power in the hands of a few state-sanctioned entities, transforming what could have been a decentralized, censorship-resistant payment layer into an extension of the traditional, centralized financial system. The Act's framework is fundamentally antithetical to the principles of openness and permissionless innovation that have defined the digital asset space.

Ultimately, the U.S. is creating a bifurcated global market. While the Act provides regulatory clarity for a conservative, innovation-stifling form of digital money, it compels more ambitious and creative projects to seek refuge in more accommodating jurisdictions. This offshore exodus of talent and capital is a significant strategic blunder. The U.S. is not leading the stablecoin revolution; it is actively ceding its leadership role by choosing to regulate the past rather than innovate for the future.

In conclusion, the GENIUS Act is a masterpiece of legislative misdirection. Under the guise of stability and security, it imposes a double standard so profound that it smothers innovation at its birth. It is an act of regulatory hypocrisy at the highest level, demanding 100% reserves from digital money while the traditional banking system operates with virtually none. This legislation is not building a new financial future; it is a defensive wall around the existing one, ensuring that the promise of truly better digital money remains a casualty of political expediency and entrenched power.

Chapter 17: Directed Digital Asset Regulation We Need (not just what Wyoming wants)

"JP Morgan always has higher capital liquidity, that is partially to make up for mistake and problems and obviously is a tough economy. We support and oversight committee…"

Jamie Dimon[20]

The discourse surrounding digital asset regulation often presents a false dichotomy: either a laissez-faire approach that risks systemic instability or a heavy-handed, restrictive framework that stifles innovation. In this crucial moment, two legislative models—the **GENIUS Act** and the **Model Law for Digital Assets (MLDA)**—offer starkly different visions for the future of the digital economy. The GENIUS Act represents a top-down, prudential approach rooted in traditional financial thinking, while the MLDA provides a bottom-up, flexible, and comprehensive framework designed to evolve with the very technology it seeks to govern. This chapter will argue that the MLDA provides a more robust and forward-looking foundation for a healthy digital asset ecosystem, one that builds resilience into the system itself rather than simply protecting the old system from the new.

---

[20] Staff (2025). "Liquidity Quotes." Briany Quote at https://www.brainyquote.com/topics/liquidity-quotes.

The GENIUS Act, while a significant step as one of the U.S.'s first federal digital asset legislations, is fundamentally a product of legacy financial thinking. Its primary focus is on "payment stablecoins" and it defines this category very narrowly, mandating a 1:1 fiat-backed model. This prescriptive approach is understandable from a risk-averse perspective, as it takes a known, regulated financial instrument—the bank deposit or Treasury—and tokenizes it. However, this narrow focus is also its greatest weakness. It overlooks the vast diversity of digital assets and stability mechanisms, effectively creating a regulatory cul-de-sac that excludes anything beyond a tokenized debit card. The "genius" of this act, it seems, is in its ability to protect the existing financial system by simply excluding the majority of innovative digital assets from its purview.

Conversely, the MLDA presents a fundamentally different philosophical underpinning. Instead of starting with a narrow, traditional instrument, it begins with a broad and flexible classification system for all digital assets. This "bottom-up" approach recognizes that the digital asset landscape is constantly changing and that a rigid legal framework is destined for obsolescence. By providing a comprehensive taxonomy for tokens ranging from Utility to Stablecoins and even Memecoins, the MLDA creates a scaffolding for regulation that can be adapted and expanded through legislative processes. This inherent flexibility is crucial for a regulatory framework that is meant to last beyond the next market cycle, allowing a nation to participate in the full spectrum of the digital economy.

The quote from Jamie Dimon—"JP Morgan always has higher capital liquidity, that is partially to make up for mistakes and problems and obviously is a tough economy. We support and oversight committee…"—serves as a poignant reminder of the enduring principles of responsible finance. Dimon's words highlight the importance of building in resilience and having oversight to manage risks and mistakes. While the GENIUS Act attempts to apply these principles to a tiny sliver of the digital asset space, the MLDA takes a more ambitious and ultimately more effective route. It seeks to build liquidity, accountability, and resilience *into the very structure of the digital asset ecosystem itself.* This means acknowledging and regulating the diverse, innovative models of stability and utility, rather than simply outlawing them and hoping they don't cause a problem.

The following sections will delve into a detailed comparison of these two legislative models across several critical areas. We will explore their differing approaches to asset classification, KYC/AML frameworks, registration philosophies, systemic protections, and international outlook. By examining these distinctions, we will demonstrate why the MLDA is not just a more permissive law, but a more responsible and future-proof piece of legislation that a nation would need to secure its place in the global digital economy.

Scope, Philosophy, and Flexibility of Classification

At its core, the GENIUS Act is built on a narrow, "top-down" philosophy of classification. Its primary concern is the stability of the financial system, and to achieve this, it creates a highly specific category for "payment stablecoins." This category is defined by a rigid set of criteria: the stablecoin must be 1:1 backed by fiat currency (USD) or short-term U.S. Treasuries. This approach is born from a desire for simplicity and certainty, applying the familiar rules of a bank deposit to a new technology. While this provides a clear pathway for a specific type of asset, it simultaneously creates a regulatory dead end for any other model, such as those that rely on different reserve assets, decentralized governance, or algorithmic stability mechanisms. The law dictates what is permissible, rather than creating a framework that can adapt to what is possible.

The MLDA, on the other hand, embraces a "bottom-up" philosophy, starting with a broad recognition of the diverse nature of digital assets. Rather than focusing on a single type, it establishes a comprehensive categorization system that includes everything from Utility and Security Tokens to Native Tokens and Stablecoins. This wide-net approach acknowledges that the digital asset space is not a monolith and that different assets serve different economic functions. By classifying them, the MLDA provides a foundation for tailored regulation. For instance, a Utility Token might require different consumer protections than a Security Token, and a Stablecoin might need different oversight mechanisms than a Native Token. This framework is about understanding and organizing the ecosystem, not just isolating a small part of it.

This inherent flexibility is most evident in the MLDA's approach to stablecoins. While the GENIUS Act mandates a single, prescriptive model, the MLDA's definition of a stablecoin is far more encompassing. It requires backing by auditable reserves and a supply control mechanism, but it explicitly permits three different models: a 1:1 asset model, an algorithmic model, or a maturity model for value vesting. This is the crucial distinction that allows for innovation. The MLDA recognizes that different stability mechanisms might be viable and that a forward-looking regulatory framework must be open to these possibilities. Instead of killing innovation, it aims to understand, regulate, and potentially even strengthen it, positioning the adopting nation to lead in the development of new, more resilient financial technologies.

Regulation of Wallets and Enhanced KYC/AML Frameworks

The GENIUS Act's approach to Know Your Customer (KYC) and Anti-Money Laundering (AML) is focused on centralized, institutional players. It mandates strict compliance for Permitted Payment Stablecoin Issuers (PPSIs) and Digital Asset Service Providers (DASPs), which include exchanges and some custodial wallets. The underlying logic is that by regulating the on-ramps and off-ramps to the traditional financial system, you can effectively combat illicit activity. However, this leaves a significant blind spot: non-custodial or peer-to-peer transactions. The law does not impose direct KYC requirements on all wallet operators, meaning that once a user obtains a stablecoin from a compliant issuer, their subsequent peer-to-peer activities using a non-custodial wallet may fall outside the direct regulatory net, making it difficult to trace the flow of illicit funds.

The MLDA takes a far more comprehensive and direct approach to this challenge. Section 6.4 is a groundbreaking provision that explicitly states, "All wallets must have a KYC policy in place to service citizens of [INSERT COUNTRY NAME HERE]." This shifts the regulatory burden from just the centralized issuers and exchanges to the wallet providers themselves, even those that are non-custodial. The philosophy here is that the software interface itself, as the point of access for citizens, is a key component of the financial ecosystem and must have accountability. This creates a much broader and more comprehensive net against illicit activities, as it aims to capture and verify the identity of the user at the point of interaction with the wallet, regardless of whether they are using a centralized exchange or not.

Furthermore, the MLDA's framework is buttressed by a holistic anti-crime focus. Section 11 outlines detailed provisions against money laundering, terrorism, human trafficking, and other criminal activities, and it applies these to cryptocurrency issuers, exchanges, and wallet providers alike. By banning anonymous tokens and requiring all wallets to have a KYC policy, the MLDA aims to eliminate anonymity for its citizens in the digital asset space. While this may raise privacy concerns for some, it provides regulators and law enforcement with a far more robust set of tools for financial intelligence and crime prevention, offering a higher degree of transparency and traceability across the entire digital asset ecosystem. This is a foundational element in building a truly secure and accountable system, rather than one with inherent loopholes.

Registration Framework vs. Exclusive Licensing

The GENIUS Act's use of exclusive licensing for stablecoin issuers is a high-barrier-to-entry model designed for a select few. It requires entities to become either a bank subsidiary or a federally/state-qualified non-bank, a process that is both costly and complex. This is the model of traditional finance, where only a handful of large, well-capitalized institutions are granted the authority to issue certain financial instruments. This approach provides a clear path for banks and established financial players to enter the space, but it effectively closes the door on smaller innovators and new market entrants. The focus is not on fostering a broad ecosystem but on creating a small, highly regulated, and easily controlled one.

In sharp contrast, the MLDA’s registration framework is built on a philosophy of broad inclusion and transparency. Section 4.0 mandates that all cryptocurrencies that want to operate within the country must register for a remarkably low fee, often a few hundred dollars. This low-cost, low-barrier-to-entry system is designed to get as many players as possible into the regulatory fold. It's a pragmatic approach that recognizes that a large, transparent ecosystem is easier to monitor and understand than a small, isolated one. This encourages innovation by not imposing prohibitive costs on new projects, and it provides regulators with a wealth of data on the entire market.

This difference in philosophy extends to all parts of the MLDA. Section 6.1 requires exchanges to register for a similar low fee, and Section 10 does the same for cryptocurrency issuers. The purpose of these registration requirements is not to limit the number of participants, but to gain visibility. By having every participant, from issuers to exchanges, on a public registry, the regulatory agency can monitor the health of the entire ecosystem, collect taxes on profits, and respond to issues as they arise. This is a framework that prioritizes data collection and regulatory oversight across the entire space, rather than just on a handful of licensed stablecoin issuers. The MLDA's model is about fostering a regulated but vibrant market, while the GENIUS Act's model is about creating a small, safe, and exclusive one.

Protecting the System vs. Protecting the "Outdated"

The GENIUS Act's method of system protection is one of exclusion. It protects the traditional fiat financial system by effectively walling it off from any digital asset model that doesn't conform to a 1:1 fiat/Treasury backing. The assumption is that models like algorithmic stablecoins or those with "smart burn" features are inherently risky and should not be allowed to integrate with the existing financial system. This approach prevents potential contagion by simply prohibiting the "dangerous" new technologies. By reinforcing a "386-era" model of digital money, it creates a digital equivalent of a bank debit card—a tokenized representation of a deposit. This model offers little to no innovation in stability mechanisms and is, by its very nature, susceptible to the same inflationary pressures and central bank policies as the traditional financial system.

The MLDA takes a more forward-thinking approach to systemic protection by building resilience and accountability into the digital asset ecosystem itself. Instead of banning alternative models, it acknowledges and defines them, and then sets operational criteria for their use. For example, it explicitly allows for algorithmic and maturity models for stablecoins, but it requires them to be backed by assets, have auditable records, and employ a "supply control model." This means that an algorithmic stablecoin cannot be a "black box" but must operate under a transparent, verifiable, and regulated framework. This approach is about understanding the risks of these new models and then mitigating them, rather than simply outlawing them.

This framework allows for the emergence of "Stablecoin 2.0" models that might offer counter-inflationary mechanisms or innovative yield-bearing technologies. The MLDA's philosophy is that innovation can lead to new and robust forms of stability, and that a progressive regulatory system should not stand in the way of that. By providing a regulatory home for these diverse models, the MLDA ensures they operate under a framework of accountability and transparency. This protects the system by understanding and regulating the diversity of digital assets, rather than just protecting the existing financial system from them. It is a framework designed to build resilience into the digital asset ecosystem itself, allowing it to thrive while still ensuring accountability.

International Outlook and Adaptability

The GENIUS Act's international outlook is primarily U.S.-centric and isolating. It is a domestic law for the U.S. financial system, with a clear focus on U.S. dollar-pegged stablecoins and the authority of U.S. regulatory bodies. While it attempts to address foreign issuers, it does so by demanding they have "comparable" regulatory regimes, a vague and potentially friction-filled requirement. This creates an environment of regulatory unilateralism, where the U.S. standard is seen as the only valid one. This approach can lead to significant problems, as it risks pushing stablecoin innovation and liquidity (especially for models that don't conform to the U.S. standard) to more accommodating jurisdictions, thereby ceding international leadership in the digital asset space.

The MLDA, by its very design, is built for global applicability and adaptability. It is presented as a "Model Bill for Cryptocurrencies" for "any legislature of the world." The law uses generalized placeholders like "[INSERT COUNTRY NAME HERE]" and "[INSERT NAME OF ENTITY THERE]" to underscore its intention to be adopted and customized by various nations. This promotes the idea of regulatory harmonization, where a shared, flexible framework can be adopted by different countries, creating a more cohesive global digital economy. Instead of a unilateral approach, the MLDA proposes a collaborative one, where different countries can use the same blueprint to build their own tailored regulatory systems.

This collaborative stance is further evidenced by the MLDA's provisions for international cooperation. It allows for the recognition of registrations from other nations for derivatives and provides protections against international lawsuits for companies operating within its borders. This emphasizes that the digital asset space is inherently global and that a successful regulatory framework must be built on a foundation of international interoperability. By offering a comprehensive yet flexible model, the MLDA positions adopting nations not to be isolated players, but to be a key part of a broader, more integrated global digital economy, potentially attracting the very innovation that the GENIUS Act might inadvertently drive away.

Comprehensive Wallet Regulation and KYC Mandates

The GENIUS Act's approach to illicit finance through KYC and AML is primarily issuer-centric. It requires robust compliance from "Permitted Payment Stablecoin Issuers" (PPSIs) and "Digital Asset Service Providers" (DASPs) who deal with compliant stablecoins. This is a reactive framework that focuses on preventing illicit activity at the points where the digital asset system intersects with the traditional financial system. However, it fails to comprehensively address peer-to-peer transactions or the use of non-custodial wallets. While it gives issuers a "kill switch" for their own tokens, this does not provide law enforcement with universal access to transactions happening off-chain or between non-custodial wallets, creating a significant and exploitable gap in oversight.

The MLDA, with its universal wallet KYC mandate, takes a bold and proactive step. The law's explicit statement, "All wallets must have a KYC policy in place to service citizens," is a groundbreaking provision that extends regulatory oversight to even non-custodial wallet interfaces and software providers. This means that a user, to simply use a wallet to transact, would have to undergo a KYC process. This completely changes the landscape of financial intelligence by eliminating the anonymity that is a core feature of many digital asset transactions. The MLDA's philosophy is that to truly combat illicit finance, you must regulate the entire ecosystem, not just the entry and exit points to the traditional system.

This aggressive stance is complemented by a direct ban on anonymous tokens. Section 11 unequivocally states, "no anonymous tokens are permitted to be sold, traded, issued, or marketed in [INSERT COUNTRY NAME HERE]." This provision directly targets privacy-focused cryptocurrencies and, combined with the wallet KYC mandate, aims to create a fully transparent digital asset ecosystem for citizens. While this approach may be seen as controversial due to privacy concerns, it offers a significantly higher level of financial intelligence for law enforcement and regulators. By dedicating entire sections to combating illicit finance and requiring all participants—issuers, exchanges, and wallet providers—to implement robust procedures, the MLDA provides a far more comprehensive approach to combating financial crime across the entire digital asset landscape.

Technical Standards, Security Audits, and Blockchain Maturity Assessment

The GENIUS Act's focus on audits is primarily financial. It mandates traditional financial audits of stablecoin reserves by Public Company Accounting Oversight Board (PCAOB) registered firms. This is the familiar and time-tested approach of traditional finance, where the central concern is the financial stability of an institution. While it implicitly requires PPSIs to demonstrate operational soundness, it doesn't prescribe specific, independent technical audit or blockchain maturity standards. This is a significant omission, as the underlying technology of a digital asset is often as important to its security and reliability as its financial reserves. A financially sound stablecoin on a technically flawed blockchain is still a significant risk.

The MLDA, on the other hand, demonstrates a deeper understanding of the technical intricacies and risks inherent in blockchain technology. It moves beyond financial audits to mandate independent **security audits** for all blockchain solutions operating within the country. This means that a third-party, reputable auditing agency must verify the code and security of the underlying technology itself. This provides a critical layer of protection by ensuring that the blockchain solution is not vulnerable to hacks or exploits, which could lead to significant financial loss and systemic instability. It acknowledges that in the digital asset space, security is not just a matter of financial reserves, but also of technical integrity.

Perhaps the most unique and forward-thinking provision in the MLDA is the requirement for a **Blockchain Maturity Model (BMM) Assessment**. This is a significant and innovative requirement that ties regulatory compliance to an objective, third-party assessment of the blockchain's operational maturity, reliability, and security. By mandating that a blockchain solution pass at least the first level of assessment by a recognized international NGO, the MLDA provides a mechanism for ongoing technical due diligence and improvement. This ensures that the underlying infrastructure is robust and reliable, offering a different, yet equally vital, layer of protection beyond just financial stability. It is a framework that understands and values the technical rigor required to build a secure digital asset ecosystem.

Registration Renewal and Accountability Mechanisms

The GENIUS Act's licensing regime, while not explicitly detailed in the provided snippets, likely relies on a traditional regulatory model for renewal. This model typically involves periodic renewal processes tied to ongoing compliance with prudential and financial reporting standards. The enforcement mechanism is top-down, with federal or state regulators holding the power to revoke authorizations and levy penalties. This is a system where accountability is measured against a fixed set of financial rules and is enforced by a centralized authority. While effective in the traditional financial space, it can be rigid and slow to adapt to the dynamic and community-driven nature of the digital asset ecosystem.

The MLDA, however, introduces a more dynamic and nuanced accountability mechanism. It requires all registrations to be renewed on a 1-year basis. The renewal process is generally automatic, but not for companies with formal complaints against them. This is a key provision that empowers the public and other entities to raise concerns and triggers a regulatory review process. This model moves beyond a simple check for financial compliance and introduces a mechanism for addressing operational issues, user complaints, or other concerns that might not be captured in a standard financial audit. It creates a higher degree of ongoing scrutiny and public accountability for registered entities.

In cases where formal complaints have been filed, the MLDA establishes an *ad hoc* panel composed of cryptocurrency experts, lawyers, and academics. This independent panel is tasked with reviewing the complaint and making a recommendation to the regulatory agency regarding the renewal. This is a groundbreaking approach that incorporates expert community input into the ongoing regulatory process, creating a more dynamic and informed response. By allowing a panel of experts to weigh in on a company's fitness for renewal, the MLDA goes beyond mere financial non-compliance and ensures continuous adherence to stated operational standards and the spirit of the law. This provides a more robust and responsive framework for accountability, making it more resilient to the challenges of a rapidly evolving technological landscape.

Government Warranty and Private Financial Activity Acknowledgment

The GENIUS Act, by creating a highly regulated "payment stablecoin" framework, implicitly aims to instill a sense of public confidence. While it explicitly states that these assets are not federally insured or legal tender, the extensive regulatory oversight, reserve requirements, and licensing process can create a perception of governmental backing or assurance. This is a common feature of financial regulation—the government's role is to ensure stability and protect consumers, which in turn fosters trust. However, this implicit confidence can also create a moral hazard, where users may assume a level of security that the law does not actually guarantee.

The MLDA takes a fundamentally different and more transparent approach by explicitly defining the government's role. It includes a clear "no warranty" clause, stating, "The government of [INSERT COUNTRY NAME HERE] makes no warranty to tokens issued to which the country does not own a reserve." This is a critical disclaimer that manages public expectations and emphasizes that the government is regulating, not guaranteeing, the value or solvency of privately issued tokens. This provision prevents a potential moral hazard by making it clear that engaging with digital assets, even regulated ones, involves personal risk and is not a risk-free, government-backed activity.

Furthermore, the MLDA clearly defines the nature of digital asset engagement as a "private financial activity" and ensures that all other existing laws—concerning contracts, fraud, and business operations—remain in "FULL EFFECT." This explicit clarification is a strength. It grounds digital asset activities firmly within existing legal principles, promoting a mature understanding of risk and responsibility for all participants. By separating the role of the government as a regulator from its role as a guarantor, the MLDA creates transparent legal boundaries and fosters a more resilient and responsible ecosystem, where innovation is encouraged but individual risk is clearly understood.

Adaptability and Focus on Evolving Threats

The GENIUS Act's approach to illicit finance is largely reactive and focused on established patterns. While it addresses AML/CFT requirements for PPSIs and emphasizes their technical capability to freeze and burn tokens, its framework is more aligned with traditional financial crime prevention. It is designed to combat money laundering and sanctions evasion as they exist within the traditional system, but it is less explicit on how it would adapt to the rapidly evolving typologies of digital asset crime. This is a static approach in a dynamic environment, which risks becoming obsolete as illicit actors find new ways to exploit emerging technologies.

The MLDA, on the other hand, is built on a foundation of foresight and continuous adaptation. Its "Anti-Criminal Activity" clause is a forward-looking provision that requires all participants—issuers, exchanges, and wallet providers—to "be prepared to identify and address new and emerging threats." This is not a passive requirement but a mandate for proactive vigilance. It recognizes that the nature of criminal activity in the digital asset space is constantly changing and that the regulatory framework must be able to evolve in response.

This proactive stance is supported by a mandate for continuous monitoring and collaboration. The MLDA encourages collaboration with industry associations, law enforcement, and regulatory authorities to "share information and best practices for combating criminal activity." This creates a feedback loop where insights from the private sector and law enforcement can inform regulatory policy. Most importantly, the law includes an inherent mechanism for evolution, noting that "new provisions in this area may be added as an addendum to this law," indicating that the legal framework can be updated without requiring entirely new legislative acts. This built-in adaptability makes the MLDA a more resilient and effective tool for combating a dynamic and ever-changing threat landscape.

Conclusion

In conclusion, a comparative analysis of the GENIUS Act and the MLDA reveals a fundamental divergence in regulatory philosophy. While the GENIUS Act is a narrow, prescriptive attempt to graft traditional financial regulations onto a single, specific class of digital assets, the MLDA is a holistic, adaptive, and future-proof framework designed to foster a healthy, secure, and innovative digital economy. Its broad classification system, direct wallet-level KYC, low-barrier registration, and recognition of diverse stability mechanisms demonstrate a deep understanding of the decentralized and rapidly evolving nature of the space.

The MLDA's approach to security is a significant departure from the old model. By requiring technical security audits and a blockchain maturity assessment, it moves beyond a focus on financial reserves to build confidence in the underlying technology itself. This provides a different, yet equally vital, layer of protection that the GENIUS Act completely omits. Furthermore, its direct regulation of wallets and a clear ban on anonymous tokens provide a more comprehensive net against illicit finance than a framework that only focuses on issuers and centralized services.

The registration philosophies of the two laws highlight another critical distinction. The GENIUS Act's high-cost licensing creates a protective, insular environment for a few large players, limiting competition and innovation. In contrast, the MLDA's low-cost, broad registration framework is designed for transparency and inclusion, inviting the entire ecosystem to participate under a clear and visible regulatory regime. This approach fosters a more vibrant and competitive market, while also giving regulators the visibility they need to ensure stability.

Ultimately, the MLDA represents a choice to lead, not just to react. Its international applicability, proactive stance on evolving criminal threats, and clear acknowledgment of the private nature of digital asset activity position it as a blueprint for a nation that wants to be a global leader in the digital economy. The GENIUS Act, by prioritizing the protection of an outdated system from the new, risks pushing innovation and liquidity offshore. The MLDA, by building a resilient and accountable framework for the digital economy from the ground up, represents the regulation we truly need to guide us into the future.

Chapter 18: Forced Conservation of Dinosaurs- Forcing People to Use Dead Systems

“While digital wallets are paving the way for future payments, you still need to assess whether or not they’ll work for your business. If your target audience are less tech-savvy or you’re primarily a cash only business, it may not be worth investing too much into accepting digital payments.”

John Rampton[21]

The quote by John Rampton, while seemingly a pragmatic piece of business advice, inadvertently reveals a fundamental misunderstanding that often plagues discussions of financial innovation: the idea that technology must conform to the limitations of existing systems and user habits. This perspective suggests a passive, reactive approach, where new tools are only adopted if they fit neatly into the "dinosaur systems" of today. In the context of digital asset regulation, this very mindset is at the heart of the GENIUS Act, a legislative effort that, despite its name, seems more intent on preserving the past than on building the future. This chapter will delve into how the GENIUS Act, by design, forces the conservation

[21] Staff (2025). “Payment Quotes.” Brainy Quote at https://www.brainyquote.com/topics/payments-quotes?gad_source=1&gad_campaignid=20728013932&gclid=Cj0KCQjwhafEBhCcARIsAEGZEKIaNQRieKQafyM9I9T2uI0HbjrJjINYEf-DZPOC17KSHByQVc8MxFEaApBmEALw_wcB

of outdated financial models, ultimately stifling innovation and hindering the natural evolution of money.

The "dinosaur systems" we're referring to are the traditional financial frameworks that have dominated for decades. They are systems built around fiat currency, centralized institutions, and slow, often opaque, processes. While they have provided stability for generations, they are also prone to inherent vulnerabilities, such as inflation and systemic risk. The GENIUS Act attempts to regulate digital assets by making them conform to these very systems. It essentially takes a powerful new technology—blockchain—and uses it to create a digital version of a debit card, tying its fate directly to the weaknesses of fiat currency and the interests of incumbent financial players.

This chapter will systematically unpack the ways in which the GENIUS Act serves to entrench these outdated systems. We will first examine how the Act's prescriptive rules create a "fiat-only straitjacket" that prevents more resilient monetary models from emerging. Next, we will analyze how these mechanisms—while designed for stability—actually hinder the development of advanced "Stablecoin 2.0" concepts that could offer superior protection for consumers. Finally, we will consider the broader, long-term implications of this approach, arguing that it compromises the U.S.'s global competitiveness and disadvantages consumers by limiting their choices.

The core problem isn't that the GENIUS Act is an overly aggressive regulation; rather, it's that it's a deeply conservative one. It uses the guise of consumer protection and financial stability to reinforce the existing power structures, effectively creating a regulatory moat around the traditional financial system. This prevents new, more innovative competitors from challenging the status quo. The Act's focus is on protecting the old system *from* the new, rather than building a new system that is better and more resilient in its own right.

In essence, the GENIUS Act is a form of "forced conservation." It takes the powerful, dynamic, and rapidly evolving potential of digital assets and attempts to freeze it in a form that is palatable to a 20th-century financial framework. By doing so, it prioritizes a sense of familiar safety over the genuine innovation that could lead to a more robust, decentralized, and ultimately more stable financial future. It's a policy of backward-looking preservation in an industry that demands forward-thinking evolution.

Entrenching The Fiat-Based "Dinosaur Systems"

The GENIUS Act's core tenets effectively solidify the dominance of traditional fiat currency and its digital surrogates, reinforcing existing power structures and preventing a fundamental evolution of digital money. This isn't a coincidence; it is the logical outcome of a regulatory philosophy that views digital assets through the lens of traditional finance. By limiting what a "payment stablecoin" can be, the Act ensures that the most powerful digital representations of money in the U.S. ecosystem are simply digital facsimiles of the old system. The regulation, in this sense, is not about embracing the future but about retrofitting the past onto a new technology.

The Act mandates that "payment stablecoins" must be 1:1 backed by highly liquid, U.S. dollar-denominated assets such as cash and short-term U.S. Treasuries. This effectively restricts stablecoins to being mere digital representations of the U.S. dollar—a "blockchain version of a debit card." While this provides a sense of familiarity and "safety" to traditional finance, it inherently limits stablecoins to inherit all the vulnerabilities of fiat currency, including its susceptibility to inflation and the monetary policies of central banks. It is a regulatory straightjacket that ensures any regulated stablecoin is inextricably tied to the fate of a single, centrally controlled asset.

This prescriptive approach prevents the development of more robust stability mechanisms. It does not allow for stablecoins backed by diversified baskets of real-world assets (e.g., commodities, real estate, a broader range of global currencies) that could offer more inherent stability or act as a hedge against the depreciation of any single fiat currency. By focusing exclusively on the USD and its equivalents, the Act creates a system that, while nominally stable in relation to the dollar, is fundamentally unstable in terms of its real-world purchasing power.

A critical component of the GENIUS Act is the prohibition of paying interest or yield to stablecoin holders. This directly undercuts the potential for stablecoins to function as a more dynamic and economically integrated form of digital money. In the traditional financial system, money held in bank accounts can earn interest, providing a natural defense against inflation for savers. By banning yield on regulated stablecoins, the GENIUS Act ensures they remain essentially non-interest-bearing digital cash. This policy is a clear signal that the regulated digital money of the future must not compete with traditional banking products.

This contrasts sharply with the potential for "Stablecoin 2.0" models that could incorporate mechanisms for yield generation (e.g., through lending protocols in decentralized finance, or by holding productive assets) to offset inflation, making them more attractive as a long-term store of value beyond mere transactional utility. The Act's prohibition ensures that the digital dollar remains a static asset, unable to dynamically adjust to changing economic conditions and unable to offer a better value proposition for savers.

The stringent licensing requirements, high capital demands, and the explicit prohibition on certain types of stablecoins (like algorithmic ones) create a significant barrier to entry for new, innovative players.

The process of becoming a "Permitted Payment Stablecoin Issuer" (PPSI) is designed for large, well-capitalized institutions. It is a process that requires a level of infrastructure, legal resources, and political connections that are beyond the reach of most startups and innovative projects. This inadvertently favors large, established financial institutions and existing fiat-backed stablecoin issuers, who already possess the infrastructure and capital to comply with such a prescriptive regulatory regime.

This creates a "moat" around the existing financial system, protecting incumbents from genuine competition. It ensures that the market remains dominated by "dinosaur systems" that mirror traditional banking, stifling competition and the emergence of genuinely decentralized or diversified digital monetary systems. The Act, by design, conserves the existing power structures and hinders the very innovation that could lead to a more competitive and equitable digital financial landscape.

Hindering "Stablecoin 2.0" and Resilient Monetary Models

The very mechanisms designed by the GENIUS Act to ensure "stability" inadvertently prevent the development and effective functioning of more advanced stablecoin models that could offer superior protection for purchasing power. This is the central paradox of the legislation: in its quest for a simple, familiar form of stability, it sacrifices the opportunity to create something truly resilient and future-proof.

"Stablecoin 2.0" concepts often aim to be "designed to protect the US dollar" not just in its nominal value, but its purchasing power. This means developing mechanisms to counteract inflation. By forcing stablecoins to be 1:1 backed by the USD or its equivalents, the GENIUS Act ensures that as the USD devalues due to inflation, so too does the stablecoin. A stablecoin worth $1.00 today will still be worth $1.00 a year from now, but that $1.00 will buy less. The Act, therefore, does not protect against the erosion of value, but rather mandates that this erosion be transferred directly to the digital asset.

"Stablecoin 2.0" could explore models where the token's value is dynamically adjusted to a basket of goods, or where protocol-level mechanisms automatically adjust supply or yield to maintain real purchasing power, rather than just a fixed nominal peg to a depreciating asset. The GENIUS Act's narrow scope effectively makes such innovation impossible within the regulated U.S. ecosystem, trapping regulated stablecoins in the same inflationary cycle as the fiat currency they mirror.

While algorithmic stablecoins have faced challenges (e.g., Terra/Luna), the outright effective prohibition or severe restriction of such models under the GENIUS Act prevents the industry from iterating and developing more robust and decentralized stability mechanisms. It is a classic case of throwing the baby out with the bathwater, where the failures of one project are used as a justification to ban an entire class of innovation. This stance ignores the fact that failure is a critical part of the innovation process and that the next generation of algorithmic stablecoins could be designed to be far more resilient.

"Stablecoin 2.0" could involve hybrid models, over-collateralized by a diverse range of digital assets (not just fiat), managed by transparent, auditable smart contracts, and potentially incorporating dynamic supply adjustments or "smart burn" mechanisms (where burned tokens' value is reinvested into the system to enhance stability or acquire more backing assets) to maintain a more resilient peg. The GENIUS Act's insistence on traditional, off-chain, 1:1 fiat-backing prevents these more complex and potentially more antifragile models from operating legally as "payment stablecoins" in the U.S., ceding their development to other, more permissive jurisdictions.

Many "Stablecoin 2.0" concepts envision decentralized governance structures where token holders participate in the management and evolution of the stablecoin protocol. This distributed control can enhance transparency, auditability, and resilience. The GENIUS Act, however, emphasizes centralized issuers (Permitted Payment Stablecoin Issuers or PPSIs) with clear lines of authority, often mirroring traditional financial institutions. This approach centralizes power in the hands of a few regulated entities, which is fundamentally at odds with the decentralized ethos of the wider digital asset community.

This centralized control, while offering regulatory comfort, stifles the very decentralized innovation that could lead to more robust, self-sustaining, and potentially counter-inflationary stablecoin models. It ensures that the future of digital money remains under the control of a handful of large institutions, rather than evolving into a more open, transparent, and resilient system that is managed by a diverse community of stakeholders.

The Broader Implications: Stifled Competitiveness and Consumer Disadvantage

The outdated approach embodied by the GENIUS Act has wider ramifications for the U.S. digital asset ecosystem and its global competitiveness. By focusing on the past, the U.S. risks losing its position as a leader in financial innovation, to the detriment of both its economy and its citizens.

By creating a regulatory framework that is overly prescriptive and backward-looking, the U.S. risks falling behind other jurisdictions that adopt more flexible and innovation-friendly approaches (like the spirit of the MLDA). The global nature of digital assets means that innovation will flourish wherever it is given the freedom to do so. If "Stablecoin 2.0" models that offer genuinely new features (like inflation protection or greater decentralization) cannot thrive in the U.S., they will inevitably develop and flourish elsewhere. This could lead to a situation where the U.S. is left with "dinosaur" stablecoins while other nations lead the charge in truly advanced digital monetary systems.

This erosion of leadership is not just a matter of prestige. It could have significant economic consequences, potentially undermining the long-term dominance of the U.S. dollar in the digital age. If other nations develop superior digital assets that are more resilient to inflation and more useful for international trade, the role of the USD as the world's reserve currency could be challenged.

For consumers, the GENIUS Act's focus on fiat-backed stablecoins means limited choice and potentially no access to digital assets designed to preserve purchasing power against inflation. While a USD-pegged stablecoin offers nominal stability, it does not protect against the real-world erosion of value that fiat currencies experience over time. Consumers seeking digital alternatives that can act as a hedge against inflation or offer greater financial resilience will be forced to look outside the regulated U.S. market, exposing them to potentially greater risks in unregulated offshore ventures.

This creates a two-tiered system: one for consumers who are content with a digital debit card, and another for those who are forced to navigate the more dangerous, unregulated waters to find tools that genuinely protect their purchasing power. By failing to provide a regulated home for these more advanced stablecoin models, the Act actually disadvantages the very consumers it purports to protect.

A significant portion of the digital asset community is driven by principles of decentralization, financial inclusion, and a desire to build more resilient and equitable financial systems. The GENIUS Act's strong centralized control, traditional backing requirements, and emphasis on existing financial institutions represent a fundamental disconnect from this ethos. This alienates a vital segment of the innovative ecosystem, pushing talent, capital, and development away from the U.S. and hindering the natural evolution of digital money towards more functional and future-proof forms.

The Act, in essence, protects the "dinosaur systems" at the expense of fostering the evolution that could genuinely "protect the US dollar" in a dynamic and increasingly digital global economy. It is a classic example of a regulatory body being captured by the interests of the past, rather than embracing the potential of the future.

Conclusion

In this chapter, we've explored how the GENIUS Act, far from being a progressive piece of legislation, is a deeply conservative regulatory measure. It is an act of “forced conservation,” designed to protect existing financial institutions and fiat currency systems by trapping the digital asset ecosystem in a narrow, outdated framework. We've seen how its prescriptive rules—from the fiat-only backing mandate to the prohibition of yield—effectively turn digital assets into a mere reflection of traditional money, inheriting all of its vulnerabilities, particularly to inflation.

This backward-looking approach is a critical misstep. By rejecting more innovative models for stability, such as those that are algorithmic, diversified, or driven by decentralized governance, the GENIUS Act hinders the development of "Stablecoin 2.0" concepts that could offer consumers genuinely superior protection for their purchasing power. It is a paradox where a quest for simple, familiar stability actually prevents the emergence of truly resilient and antifragile monetary systems.

The ramifications of this approach extend far beyond the technical and financial details. By stifling innovation, the U.S. risks ceding its global leadership in the digital economy to more forward-thinking nations. It also creates a consumer disadvantage, forcing those who seek alternatives to the inflationary pressures of fiat to venture into unregulated markets, exposing them to greater risk. The Act's disconnect from the core ethos of decentralization and financial inclusion alienates a vibrant community of innovators, pushing talent and capital away.

Ultimately, the genius of any regulation lies in its ability to adapt and evolve with the technology it governs. The GENIUS Act fails this test by attempting to preserve "dinosaur systems" at the expense of future innovation. The goal of a truly effective framework should not be to protect the old, but to thoughtfully and intelligently build the new—creating a more resilient, dynamic, and inclusive financial system for the digital age.

Chapter 19: Conceptual Framework of Digital Cooperation

“If there is someone in your life who is not serving you or making you better, give yourself the permission to move on.”

Niecy Nash[22]

Niecy Nash’s quote, while intended for personal relationships, offers a powerful metaphor for our current relationship with outdated financial and regulatory systems. The "someone" in this context is the antiquated and restrictive mindset that prioritizes the preservation of "dinosaur systems" over the adoption of genuinely transformative technologies. The previous chapter highlighted how the GENIUS Act is an embodiment of this mindset, a regulatory framework that clings to the familiar at the expense of innovation. This chapter will argue that to move forward, we must "give ourselves the permission to move on" from this narrow perspective and adopt a new conceptual framework of digital cooperation—a framework that is not only a regulatory approach, but a philosophy for building a resilient, innovative, and secure digital financial ecosystem.

The central thesis of this chapter is that an effective regulatory framework must be built on the principle of constructive engagement rather than protective

[22] Staff (2025). “Permission Quotes.” Brainy Quote at https://www.brainyquote.com/topics/permission-quotes.

exclusion. It should not be a one-size-fits-all straitjacket that stifles technological progress, but a flexible, categorized scaffold that provides a home for a diverse range of digital assets. This framework must acknowledge that innovation is a process of iteration and that a regulatory body's role is not to ban new ideas, but to understand and appropriately mitigate their risks. We need a system that recognizes that a "Stablecoin 2.0" might be a critical tool for fighting inflation and protecting consumer purchasing power, a capability that a simple fiat-pegged token cannot provide.

This chapter will present a three-pronged conceptual framework designed to foster this digital cooperation. First, we will propose a categorized approach to stablecoin innovation, which moves beyond the simple 1:1 fiat peg and embraces a tiered system for regulating diverse stability mechanisms, including algorithmic and asset-backed models. This is about creating a space for "Stablecoin 2.0" to thrive, rather than pushing it into the shadows. Second, we will discuss how to safeguard federal monetary authority by explicitly preventing states from issuing their own stablecoins, thereby maintaining a unified national monetary policy while still encouraging private sector innovation.

Finally, we will outline a robust financial integrity framework based on universal KYC for all wallets and a clear ban on privacy coins. This addresses the legitimate concerns around illicit finance by eliminating anonymity at the foundational level of the digital ecosystem, thereby building a more secure and accountable system for everyone. The combination of these three elements—fostering innovation, protecting federal authority, and ensuring financial integrity—forms a cohesive and forward-looking approach that is not just a reaction to digital assets, but a proactive plan for their successful integration into our economy.

In essence, this framework is about creating a symbiotic relationship between regulation and innovation. Instead of regulators viewing themselves as gatekeepers of an old system, they can become facilitators of a new one. By moving on from the restrictive model of forced conservation, we can build a regulatory environment that is responsive, adaptable, and ultimately, better for both the economy and the consumer.

A Categorized Approach to Stablecoin Innovation (Beyond Fiat-Pegged)

Instead of a narrow focus on 1:1 fiat-backed stablecoins, a revised framework should embrace a categorized approach that allows for the innovation of "Stablecoin 2.0" models, including algorithmic and "matrix-backed" systems, with appropriate risk-calibrated regulation. This is the crucial first step in moving on from the "dinosaur systems" of the past. By creating a regulatory home for a diversity of stability mechanisms, we acknowledge that the future of digital money is not a single, monolithic entity, but a dynamic ecosystem of tools designed for different purposes and risk profiles.

Tiered Regulation for Diverse Stablecoin Models

The new framework should recognize distinct stablecoin categories beyond just "payment stablecoins." This would include three primary tiers, each with its own regulatory requirements:

- **Tier 1: Fiat-Collateralized** stablecoins would be similar to current definitions, requiring 100% reserves in high-quality, liquid fiat or short-term government securities, subject to strict audit and reporting. These would be ideal for everyday payments, where a simple and predictable peg to the national currency is paramount. The familiarity of this model would also provide a comfortable entry point for less tech-savvy users and traditional businesses.
- **Tier 2: Asset-Collateralized** stablecoins would represent a significant step forward, allowing backing by a diversified basket of assets. This could include commodities (e.g., gold, real estate indexes), a portfolio of digital assets, or even other national currencies. These "matrix-backed" stablecoins would derive stability from the complex interplay of diverse assets and a rebalancing algorithm, potentially offering a more robust hedge against the depreciation of any single currency.

Regulation for this tier would focus on the quality and liquidity of the underlying assets, transparent collateral management, and robust risk frameworks, ensuring that consumers are protected without stifling the innovative potential of this model.

- **Tier 3: Algorithmic/Hybrid** stablecoins would acknowledge the potential for decentralized stability. Instead of an outright ban, this tier would be regulated with a focus on mitigating the specific risks associated with these models. This includes mandatory capitalization requirements, such as over-collateralization or dedicated stability funds, and strict transparency rules that require open-source code and real-time on-chain audits. Furthermore, these stablecoins would be subject to mandatory stress testing under various market conditions to assess their resilience, along with clear, pre-defined contingency plans for de-pegging events and orderly unwinds to protect users.

To enable stablecoins to "beat inflation" and offer reasonable yields, the revised act should permit and regulate stablecoin issuers to manage their reserves through diversified investment strategies, akin to traditional financial instruments, provided transparency and risk management are paramount. Unlike the GENIUS Act's ban on interest, a new law would allow issuers to generate reasonable yield on their reserves through prudently managed, multifaceted index funds, mutual funds, or other "basket of goods methodologies." This permits stablecoins to preserve or even grow purchasing power, acting as a true store of value that provides a much-needed defense for savers against the ongoing erosion of value in fiat currency.

This framework would not be a free-for-all. Strict oversight of investment strategies would be a non-negotiable requirement. Regulations would define permissible asset classes, diversification requirements, and risk limits, and mandate regular, independent audits of these investment portfolios to ensure transparency and prevent reckless speculation with user funds. The focus would be on conservative, yield-generating strategies that align with stability goals, providing a robust, regulated, and yield-bearing option for consumers, while simultaneously creating a viable and innovative product for issuers.

Safeguarding Federal Monetary Authority and Preventing "Company Money" by States

The proposed framework must explicitly prevent states from issuing their own stablecoins that could undermine the U.S. federal government's constitutional power to coin money, while allowing private sector innovation. This is a critical provision that maintains the integrity of the national monetary system and prevents the kind of economic fragmentation that plagued the nation in its earliest days.

The U.S. Constitution grants the federal government the sole power to "coin Money" and "regulate the Value thereof." This is a fundamental principle of our nation's economic stability, designed to prevent a patchwork of different currencies and the economic chaos that would ensue. The historical issues with state-issued "company money" during the Articles of Confederation era, which led to trade barriers and a lack of trust in the national economy, serve as a potent warning. State-issued stablecoins, particularly those intended for mandatory use within a state or offering preferential treatment to state residents, could directly violate this fundamental principle, creating a fractured monetary system that challenges the authority of the U.S. dollar.

The revised act should explicitly prohibit state governments (and their agencies or state-chartered entities if acting as a governmental rather than purely private entity) from issuing stablecoins that are designed to be the sole or mandatory means of payment for state taxes, fees, or services. It would also prohibit them from granting exclusive or preferential economic rights or privileges to state residents or businesses not available to others using federal currency. The goal here is to prevent a state from attempting to create a separate monetary system within its borders, distinct from the U.S. dollar, thereby directly challenging federal monetary policy and fragmenting the national economy.

The law must clearly distinguish between private actors (corporations, DAOs, individuals) who may issue private currencies or stablecoins, and state governments. While private stablecoins would be regulated under the new federal framework, state entities are subject to the constitutional limitations on monetary issuance. This allows for healthy private sector innovation in digital currency without fragmenting the national monetary system. By creating this clear distinction, the framework empowers private entities to innovate, while at the same time preserving the crucial and long-established role of the federal government as the sole authority on monetary policy.

Universal KYC for Wallets and a Ban on Privacy Coins

To ensure financial integrity and combat illicit activities, a robust framework must extend KYC requirements to all wallets servicing U.S. citizens and implement a clear ban on privacy coins. This is a foundational step in building a secure and accountable digital ecosystem. By eliminating the blind spots that exist in current regulations, we can provide law enforcement and regulators with the tools they need to prevent the use of digital assets for crime.

As seen in the MLDA, a fundamental shift in regulatory approach should be a strict requirement for all wallet providers (custodial and non-custodial) servicing U.S. citizens to implement robust Know

Your Customer (KYC) procedures. This includes a clear identity verification process that requires government-issued ID, name, address, and nationality for all users. Wallet providers would also need to register with a designated federal agency (e.g., FinCEN or a new digital asset regulator) and be subject to regular audits of their KYC/AML compliance. The goal is to eliminate financial anonymity within the U.S. digital asset ecosystem, enhancing the ability of law enforcement to combat illicit finance and build a system that is as secure and accountable as the traditional financial system.

To further bolster anti-money laundering and counter-terrorism financing efforts, the revised act should explicitly ban the issuance, sale, trading, or holding of "privacy coins" within the United States. This would require a clear legal definition, generally encompassing cryptocurrencies designed with enhanced anonymity features (e.g., obscuring transaction amounts, senders, or recipients) that inherently hinder KYC/AML efforts. The ban would necessitate mechanisms for exchanges and wallet providers to delist and prevent transactions involving such coins for U.S. citizens, with penalties for non-compliance. While privacy features can be valuable in some contexts, their potential for illicit use at a foundational level necessitates this measure for national security and financial integrity.

Acknowledging concerns about individual privacy, the act should clarify that the focus is on financial transparency for AML/CTF purposes, not on intrusive surveillance of legitimate activities. The intent is to ensure that digital assets cannot become untraceable conduits for crime, aligning with existing regulations in traditional finance. By adopting this stance, the framework provides a far more secure and accountable digital asset ecosystem, which will ultimately increase trust and potentially accelerate mainstream adoption. The balance struck here is a critical one, prioritizing the safety and security of the broader financial system while still allowing for the private and legitimate use of digital assets.

Conclusion

In this chapter, we have moved beyond the critique of outdated regulations and have instead proposed a comprehensive conceptual framework for digital cooperation. We've argued that just as Niecy Nash's quote suggests, it is time to give ourselves permission to move on from a regulatory mindset that serves neither innovation nor security. The GENIUS Act's approach of "forced conservation" is not sustainable, and it is a path that will ultimately lead to the U.S. ceding its leadership role in the global digital economy.

The framework we've outlined is not an abandonment of regulation, but a mature and forward-thinking evolution of it. By adopting a tiered approach to stablecoin innovation, we create a regulated and transparent home for "Stablecoin 2.0" models that can offer real-world value, such as protection against inflation. By safeguarding the federal government's constitutional power to coin money, we ensure that a single, unified national economy is preserved, while still empowering private innovators to build the future.

Finally, by mandating universal KYC for wallets and banning privacy coins, we address the legitimate concerns of illicit finance head-on. This comprehensive approach to financial integrity eliminates the anonymity that has been a long-standing criticism of digital assets and replaces it with a transparent, accountable system that can be trusted by law enforcement and consumers alike.

This conceptual framework of digital cooperation is a path forward that balances innovation, security, and integrity. It is an approach that acknowledges the power of digital assets, understands their potential, and works to guide them toward a constructive role in our economy. It is an opportunity for the U.S. to not just keep pace with the digital revolution, but to lead it by creating a regulatory environment that is not afraid to give itself permission to move on.

Conclusion

"The lies the government and media tell are amplifications of the lies we tell ourselves. To stop being conned, stop conning yourself."

James Wolcott[23]

In the preceding chapters, we have navigated a critical juncture in financial history, one defined by the tension between the established order and the disruptive force of digital innovation. The central conflict of this book has been a stark contrast in regulatory philosophies: the backward-looking approach of the GENIUS Act, a legislative attempt at what we have termed "forced conservation," versus a forward-thinking framework of "digital cooperation." This conflict is not merely academic; it represents a fundamental choice that will determine the future competitiveness and resilience of our financial systems in the digital age.

The GENIUS Act, despite its seemingly progressive title, emerged from a mindset of institutional preservation. It is a deeply conservative piece of legislation that, in its effort to manage risk, chose to simply wall off the traditional financial system from any digital asset that did not conform to its narrow, outdated model. It is not an act of malice, but rather a

[23] Staff (2025). "Conned Quotes." Brainy Quote at https://www.brainyquote.com/topics/conned-quotes.

profound failure of imagination, using the powerful new tools of blockchain technology to create a regulatory system built on a 20th-century foundation.

The most glaring manifestation of this failure is the Act’s "fiat-only" straitjacket. By mandating that all regulated "payment stablecoins" must be 1:1 backed by U.S. dollar-denominated assets, the law effectively limits them to being little more than a digital debit card. This prescriptive approach ensures that these tokens inherit all the vulnerabilities of fiat currency, including its susceptibility to inflation and central bank policies, thereby trapping them in the same "dinosaur system" they were meant to transcend.

This myopic focus on fiat-pegged models actively suppresses the development of more resilient financial instruments. Throughout our analysis, we’ve highlighted the potential of "Stablecoin 2.0" models—digital assets designed not just for nominal stability, but for the protection of purchasing power against inflation. These models, which could leverage diversified asset baskets, algorithmic stability mechanisms, and decentralized governance, are effectively outlawed by the GENIUS Act, preventing the industry from iterating and building genuinely antifragile forms of digital money.

In stark contrast, the Model Law for Digital Assets (MLDA) and the conceptual framework it inspired offer a superior path. The MLDA represents a philosophy of digital cooperation, built on the principle that the role of regulation is not to stifle innovation but to guide it. It is a bottom-up, flexible, and comprehensive system that provides a scaffold for a diverse array of digital assets, acknowledging that the digital economy is a dynamic ecosystem that cannot be governed by a single, rigid set of rules.

This forward-thinking philosophy forms the basis of the comprehensive framework we proposed in Chapter 19. The first pillar of this framework is a **tiered approach to stablecoin regulation**, which provides a regulated home for Fiat-Collateralized (Tier 1), Asset-Collateralized (Tier 2), and Algorithmic/Hybrid (Tier 3) stablecoins. This tiered system is calibrated to the specific risks of each model, fostering innovation while ensuring that consumer protections and financial integrity remain paramount.

The second pillar addresses a crucial constitutional concern. By explicitly safeguarding the **federal government's monetary authority**, the framework prevents states from issuing their own stablecoins that could fragment the national monetary system and undermine the U.S. dollar. This is a vital step in maintaining economic unity, while simultaneously empowering the private sector to innovate freely within a clear and consistent regulatory environment.

The third and final pillar establishes a robust system for **financial integrity**. This is achieved through a mandate for universal Know Your Customer (KYC) procedures for all wallet providers and a clear, unambiguous ban on privacy coins. This approach removes the anonymity that has long been a source of criticism for digital assets and provides law enforcement with the necessary tools to combat illicit finance, thereby building a more transparent and trustworthy ecosystem for all participants.

Ultimately, the choice before us is a profound one. We can choose the path of the GENIUS Act, which leads to a stifled and backward-looking digital ecosystem, where the U.S. risks ceding its global leadership in financial innovation to more nimble nations. Or, we can choose the path of digital cooperation, which promises a future of a more dynamic, resilient, and inclusive financial system.

This decision goes beyond the technical details of a specific bill. It is a choice about a fundamental regulatory philosophy. It asks whether we will view digital assets as a threat to be contained or as an opportunity to be harnessed. It challenges us to heed the wisdom of Niecy Nash's quote and "give ourselves the permission to move on" from the outdated systems and mindsets that are no longer serving us.

The future of finance is not a conservation project; it is a creation project. It requires a willingness to embrace complexity, to learn from past failures, and to build a framework that is not afraid of the future. The conceptual framework of digital cooperation is not an end, but a beginning—a blueprint for a financial system that is not only secure and stable, but also innovative, inclusive, and capable of meeting the challenges of the 21st century.

By implementing these principles, we can move beyond the "dinosaur systems" and create a digital financial ecosystem that is robust, trustworthy, and a source of genuine prosperity for generations to come.

Appendix 1: Sample US Law Based on DCBAS Model Law

The Digital Asset Innovation and Stability Act (DAISA)

A Bill to Foster Responsible Innovation, Ensure Financial Stability, and Protect Consumers in the Digital Asset Economy.

Be it enacted by the Senate and House of Representatives of the United States of America in Congress assembled.

Section 1: Categories of Stable Digital Assets and Oversight

(a) Purpose: This Act establishes a comprehensive framework for the classification, regulation, and oversight of stable digital assets in the United States, fostering innovation while ensuring market integrity and consumer protection.

(b) Definitions:

- **Stable Digital Asset (SDA):** A digital asset designed to maintain a stable value relative to a specified reference asset or basket of assets.
- **Fiat-Referenced Stable Digital Asset (FR-SDA):** An SDA designed to maintain a stable value relative to one or more fiat currencies (e.g., USD, EUR).

- **Treasury-Referenced Stable Digital Asset (TR-SDA):** An SDA designed to maintain a stable value primarily through backing by U.S. Treasury securities.
- **Algorithmic/Matrix-Backed Stable Digital Asset (AMB-SDA):** An SDA that maintains its stability through programmatic adjustments of supply and demand, or a diversified, dynamically managed basket of assets (e.g., commodities, other digital assets, real-world assets), without 1:1 direct fiat or Treasury backing.
- **Inflation-Resilient Stable Digital Asset (IR-SDA):** Any SDA that, through its design and management, demonstrates an average annual appreciation or value preservation that at least matches the U.S. Consumer Price Index (CPI) over a three-year rolling period. This will be determined by independent, third-party audits.
- **On-Ramp/Off-Ramp (OROR) System:** Any entity or service that facilitates the exchange of fiat currency for digital assets, or digital assets for fiat currency.
- **Blockchain Maturity Model (BMM):** The global standard for assessing the trustworthiness of blockchain solutions, as defined and maintained by the Government Blockchain Association (GBA).

- **Central Bank Enacted Digital Currency (CBEDC):** A digital form of a country's fiat currency, issued and backed by its central bank (e.g., the Federal Reserve for the U.S.).

(c) Regulatory Authority: The Secretary of the Treasury, in consultation with the Federal Reserve, the Securities and Exchange Commission (SEC), and the Commodity Futures Trading Commission (CFTC), shall designate primary regulators for each category of SDA, based on their underlying design and risk profile. This includes issuing necessary rules and guidance.

(d) Classification and Registration:

- All entities intending to issue or facilitate the use of an SDA in the United States shall register with the designated primary regulator, providing detailed information on their SDA's design, backing mechanism, and operational model.
- The designated regulator shall classify each SDA into one of the categories defined in subsection (b) or a new category established under this Act.

Section 2: Strict Regulations for Stable Digital Assets

(a) Fiat-Referenced and Treasury-Referenced SDAs (FR-SDAs & TR-SDAs):

- **Strict Reserve Requirements:** FR-SDAs and TR-SDAs shall maintain 100% reserves in cash, cash equivalents, or short-term U.S. Treasury securities, held in segregated accounts with regulated depository institutions. These reserves shall be subject to daily attestations and monthly independent audits by Public Company Accounting Oversight Board (PCAOB) registered accounting firms, publicly verifiable.
- **Prohibition on Yield (Limited):** FR-SDAs and TR-SDAs may not directly offer interest or yield to holders solely for holding the stablecoin, to prevent misrepresentation as a deposit-bearing instrument. Reasonable operational fees for services are permitted.
- **Transparent Redemption:** Issuers shall maintain clear, public redemption policies guaranteeing timely 1:1 redemption for the underlying fiat currency or Treasury equivalent.

(b) Algorithmic/Matrix-Backed Stable Digital Assets (AMB-SDAs):

- **Comprehensive Auditing and Stress Testing:** Issuers of AMB-SDAs shall be subject to rigorous, independent annual financial and technical audits. These audits must assess:
    1. **Algorithmic Robustness:** A detailed review of the algorithm's code,

economic model, and stability mechanisms.

2. **Reserve Management:** Verification of all underlying assets, their valuation methodologies, and the integrity of smart contracts governing them.
3. **Stress Testing:** Mandatory stress tests simulating extreme market volatility, de-pegging events, and significant liquidity shocks, with results publicly disclosed.
4. **Contingency Planning:** Documented and tested plans for managing and unwinding in the event of a severe de-pegging or systemic failure.

- **Capital Buffers:** AMB-SDAs shall maintain dynamic capital buffers or over-collateralization ratios, as determined by the designated regulator, sufficient to absorb potential losses from market volatility and algorithmic adjustments.
- **Maturity Model Assessment:** Within two years of initial registration, all AMB-SDAs must undergo and pass at least Level 1 of the Blockchain Maturity Model (BMM) Assessment published by the Government Blockchain Association (GBA), and regularly update their assessment level as part of ongoing compliance.

(c) Inflation-Resilient Stable Digital Assets (IR-SDAs):

- **Yield Generation Through Managed Funds:** IR-SDAs are specifically permitted to generate reasonable yield through prudent management models, including multi-faceted index funds, mutual funds, or other "basket of goods methodologies," provided these are transparent, auditable, and adhere to strict risk management guidelines set by the designated regulator.
- **Transparency and Disclosure:** Issuers of IR-SDAs must clearly disclose their investment strategies, risk profiles, and historical performance relative to inflation, in plain language, to all prospective holders.

Section 3: On-Ramp/Off-Ramp Systems and Banking Integration

(a) On-Ramp/Off-Ramp (OROR) System Requirements:

- **Operating Reserve and Operational Resilience (OROR) Requirement:** All OROR systems (e.g., entities like Tether and Circle) facilitating fiat-crypto conversion for U.S. citizens must maintain sufficient liquidity and operational resilience to handle sudden surges in redemption requests and ensure seamless transitions between fiat and digital assets. This includes, but is not limited to:

1. **Liquid Reserves:** Maintaining highly liquid reserves in regulated financial institutions equal to their outstanding fiat liabilities.
2. **Operational Capacity:** Demonstrating robust technological infrastructure, cybersecurity protocols, and redundancy plans to ensure continuous operation.
3. **Real-Time Monitoring:** Implementing real-time monitoring and reporting systems to regulators regarding their liquidity levels and operational status.

- **Federal Registration and Oversight:** OROR systems shall be federally registered as Money Service Businesses (MSBs) under FinCEN and subject to oversight by the designated primary regulator, with strict KYC/AML/CFT compliance.

(b) Central Bank Enacted Digital Currencies (CBEDCs) and Banking Integration:

- **Federal Reserve Approval for Bank Usage:** Insured Depository Institutions (banks and credit unions) operating in the United States are **only permitted to use or integrate Stable Digital Assets (SDAs) that are explicitly approved by the Federal Reserve** for such purposes.

- **CBEDC Priority:** The Federal Reserve's approval framework shall prioritize its own Central Bank Enacted Digital Currencies (CBEDCs) as the preferred stable digital asset for bank integration, once such CBEDCs are fully developed and implemented.
- **Limited Private SDA Approval for Banks:** Any private SDA approved for bank usage must demonstrate exceptional stability, regulatory compliance, interoperability, and alignment with national monetary policy objectives, as determined solely by the Federal Reserve.

Section 4: Prohibitions and Wallet Requirements

(a) Prohibition on State-Issued Stable Digital Assets:

- **Federal Monetary Authority:** No State, territory, or political subdivision of the United States, nor any agency or entity acting on their behalf, shall issue, mint, or endorse any Stable Digital Asset that is intended to serve as a mandatory medium of exchange within their jurisdiction, or that attempts to create a distinct monetary system separate from the U.S. dollar.
- **Private Entity Issuance:** Stable Digital Assets in the United States shall be issued solely by private entities duly registered and compliant with federal law. This preserves the federal

government's exclusive constitutional power to coin money and regulate its value.

(b) Wallet Know Your Customer (KYC) Requirement:

- **Universal KYC:** Any individual or entity providing digital asset wallet services to citizens or residents of the United States, whether custodial or non-custodial, must implement robust Know Your Customer (KYC) procedures. This includes obtaining and verifying:
    1. Government-issued identification.
    2. Full legal name and date of birth.
    3. Physical address and nationality.
    4. The wallet address(es associated with the user.
- **Wallet Provider Registration:** All wallet providers servicing U.S. citizens must register with FinCEN as MSBs and adhere to all applicable Anti-Money Laundering (AML) and Countering the Financing of Terrorism (CFT) regulations.

(c) Prohibition on Privacy Coins:

- **Ban on Anonymous Tokens:** No anonymous tokens or "privacy coins" (digital assets designed primarily to obscure transaction details, sender, or recipient identity through cryptographic means) shall be issued, sold, traded, or marketed within the United States.

- **Holding Prohibition:** Citizens, residents, or contractors within the United States are prohibited from holding such anonymous tokens. This provision is designed to enhance financial transparency and combat illicit activities.
- **Traceability Requirement:** All digital asset transactions conducted or facilitated within the United States must be traceable and adhere to established AML/CFT standards.

Section 5: Legacy Tokens and General Provisions

(a) Continued Operation of Existing Tokens:

- Any digital asset or stablecoin in circulation prior to the enactment of this Act that is already properly branded and widely adopted may continue to operate, provided it fully complies with the applicable requirements laid out in this Act based on its classification.
- Issuers of such existing tokens shall apply for classification and registration within six (6) months of this Act's effective date and submit to all applicable audits and requirements.

(b) General Protections:

- Cryptocurrency companies operating within the United States will be given necessary protections from international lawsuits, and, unless otherwise specified in the operational contracts and documents of the organization, shall be construed that all operations within the United States will be operating under the laws of the United States.

- The U.S. Government makes no warranty as to the value of privately issued digital assets. Purchase or use of any digital asset is a private financial activity. All existing laws concerning contracts, fraud, and other business operations are in full effect unless explicitly superseded by this Act.

(c) Enactment Clause: This Act shall take effect [INSERT DATE HERE, e.g., 180 days after enactment].

(d) Severability Clause: If any provision of this Act, or the application thereof to any person or circumstance, is held invalid, the remainder of the Act, and the application of such provision to other persons or circumstances, shall not be affected thereby.

Made in United States
Orlando, FL
04 November 2026

90202583R00154